# PUT SOME FLESH ONTO THE BONES

# PUT SOME FLESH ONTO THE BONES

Discovering the ancestors on a family tree
are real people who can be related to

## RON DEARING

Written and published by

Byron Dearing

Adelaide, South Australia

dearing@iinet.net.au

First edition 2021

ISBN 978-1-008-99025-8

Non-fiction – pioneers, early Australian – biography – genealogy

Printed by Lulu.com

## DEDICATION

This book is dedicated to my son Todd, my daughter Michelle, and my grandchildren Kaelie, Mickey, Jayden and Chloe. After reading this book, may they understand their ancestors a little more, appreciate the people that they were, the challenges they met, the sacrifices they made, and how their endeavours built a life in Australia for their family and for future generations.

*If we know where we came from, we may better know where to go. If we know who we came from, we may better understand who we are.*

*- Anonymous*

# CONTENTS

# PREFACE

Sergeant Andrew Russell was the first Australian to die in the Afghanistan conflict against the Taliban in February 2002. His death was the first Australian military death for thirty years since the Vietnam War. "Drew," as he was known by his fellow soldiers, was a member of the elite Special Air Service Regiment. He had been in the army for sixteen years and had previously been deployed in Iraq, Kuwait and East Timor.

Sergeant Russell had died from injuries sustained when his long-range patrol vehicle ran over an anti-tank mine in the aptly named "Desert of Death" (near the "Desert of Hell"), one of the most unforgiving places on Earth. A US medical team parachuted in to stabilize him, but despite their desperate efforts in transferring him by helicopter to the US medical facility at Kandahar, he succumbed to his injuries. He left a young wife and an eleven days old daughter (whom he never got to see).

Andrew was the nephew of some of our dearest friends. We had seen him as a child grow up to a teenager and then a young man fanatical about anything military. At the time of his death, my wife and I were holidaying in Western Australia. Upon our return home to Adelaide, I visited the State Library of South Australia where they had a newspaper reading room. (Few newspapers were available to read on the internet then.) Andrew had grown up in Adelaide, so I was interested to see how the Adelaide press had reported the death and also to peruse the death and funeral notices.

Having found and read the information I had been seeking, I glanced at my watch. I had about an hour to fill in before lunch. Within the library I noticed a sign indicating the "Family History" collection. I could spend an hour there and then have my lunch.

I commenced searching for my mother's side of the family, as I did have some limited knowledge about that family previously given to me by my mother. I casually browsed through various birth, death and marriage records. I soon found a few results – names that were familiar to me. However, going further back I was to discover names that were new to me. With some assistance from the librarian, I was even able to find records of the ship on which my mother's Bartlett family had immigrated from England to Australia. This was interesting stuff. A further recorded notation actually showed receipt of the amount in English pounds that my direct ancestor had paid for each family member for the voyage to immigrate to Australia. There it was in black and white in front of me – the names of the family and the actual fares that were paid in the transaction made *150 years ago*. This to me was fascinating information. I was blown away. From that moment I was hooked on the pursuit of finding about my family history.

I glanced at my watch to check to see if it was time for my lunch. It was 4-30 p.m. It would go down on record to be the first time a Dearing had ever missed their lunch!

Eight years later:

I had just become a member of the Fleurieu Peninsula Family History Group Inc. of South Australia and was attending my first meeting at their meeting place at Christies Beach. For the previous eight years I had conducted thorough and painstaking research, spending countless hours often till the early morning, drinking too much coffee and accumulating various names of my ancestors and their dates of birth and death. Almost every possible record had been pursued – examining numerous B.D.M. records (births, deaths and marriage), parish records, census returns, wills, newspapers, diaries, directories and using the website of Family Search (the Church of the Latter-Day Saints).

After undertaking such a thorough search, I had managed to trace my family tree back to about 1600, having over 2,000 substantiated names and dates. I regretted that I had been unable to find a single convict among my direct relatives. As an Australian I wish I had. (Jack Thompson, the Australian film star, once said on the "Who do you think you are" television program that for an Australian to have a convict as an ancestor was like having "Australian royalty.")

Senior members of the Family History Group seemed to be suitably impressed when I showed them my quite comprehensive family tree with so many names and dates. (Normally new members joining the organization had minimum ancestors on their family tree, or even none at all if they hadn't commenced the research of their tree.)

Feeling relatively pleased with myself, I was acknowledging the praise bestowed upon me for my efforts. One senior member of the Group however pulled me aside. "Ron," she said, "You must *put some flesh onto the bones.*" In an instant I had an inkling as to what she was suggesting, however I feebly blurted back, "What do you mean?" She continued, "Your extensive family tree certainly is top-class. It is however really just a list of boring names and dates. Every one of these names has a story to tell. You must find out where they were born and lived, their family life, their occupation, their character, the challenges they faced, what they achieved, the mistakes that they made, their shortcomings. Make them into real people."

Now I clearly understood. I thanked her for her advice. (I immediately made a mental note to also include finding out the reason why many of my ancestors came to Australia, something that she hadn't mentioned.) After eight years of back-breaking research, I now had a new task: to find out about these ancestors, these "names and dates," to make them into real people that can be related to, to *put some flesh onto the bones.*

Henry Foster

6

# 1

# HENRY FOSTER

## 1821 – 1889

# FAMILY TREE

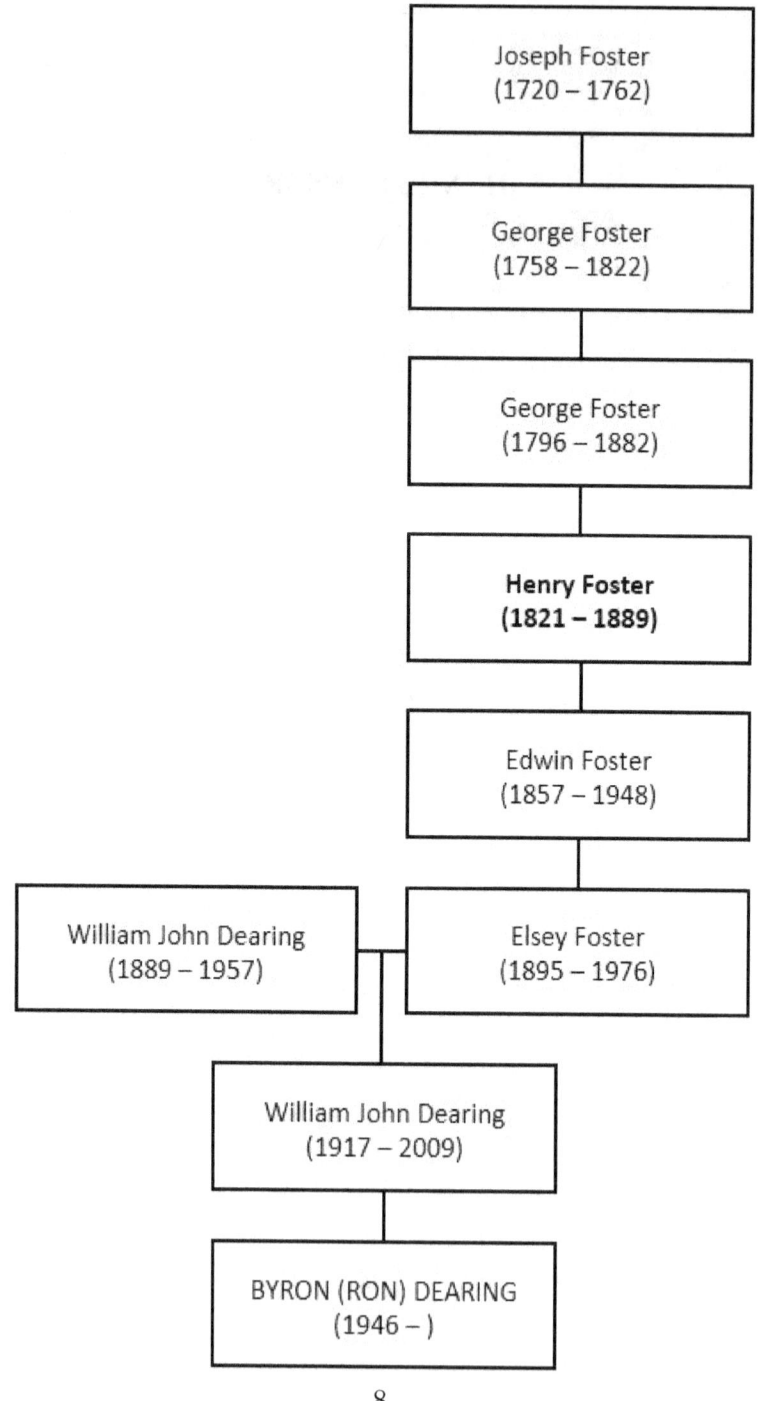

Joseph Foster
(1720 – 1762)

George Foster
(1758 – 1822)

George Foster
(1796 – 1882)

**Henry Foster
(1821 – 1889)**

Edwin Foster
(1857 – 1948)

William John Dearing
(1889 – 1957)

Elsey Foster
(1895 – 1976)

William John Dearing
(1917 – 2009)

BYRON (RON) DEARING
(1946 – )

The surname Foster is an early aberration of the word forester which is "a person who works in a forest."

The Fosters in my family have been traced back to the 1700s having come from Buckinghamshire, England. The area of Buckinghamshire where they lived was a triangle of three villages, being Hardwick, Whitchurch and Weedon which were just north of the capital Aylesbury. It was a farming community set in gentle rolling open pastures, ideal for agriculture.

Generations of Fosters had been for their lifetime agricultural labourers in that area, working not for themselves, but for lords of the manor, (known as country squires who owned the land). The squires were gentlemen who were considered gentry, gaining profits on the farms without getting their own hands dirty. The farms were worked by the agricultural labourers, who worked as tenants for little reward. The common expression of "the rich get richer, while the poor get poorer" applied.

Henry Foster was born at Weedon in 1821 to agricultural labourer George Foster and his wife Frances Cheshire. (George and Frances had both born in nearby Whitchurch). He was the eldest son of six children. He grew up in the close-knit farming community and became an agricultural labourer himself, working for the local squire on a tenanted farm. He kept ducks and geese which supplemented his income, selling them at the local market.

In 1846 Henry aged 25 married Elizabeth Lee aged 20, the daughter of a local agricultural labourer and sometimes basket-maker William Lee, at the St. Mary's Hardwick parish church. As Henry was illiterate, he signed the marriage certificate with an 'X'. The "signature" was witnessed by Henry's brother Alfred.

St. Mary's Church Hardwick

1846. Marriage solemnized at the Church in the Parish of Prestwick in the County of Bucks

| No. | When Married | Name and Surname | Age | Condition | Rank or Profession | Residence at the Time of Marriage | Father's Name and Surname | Rank or Profession of Father |
|---|---|---|---|---|---|---|---|---|
| 79 | Nov. 9 | Henry Foster | 25 | Bachelor | Labourer | Weedon | George Foster | Labourer |
| | | Elizabeth Lee | 21 | Spinster | | Weedon | William Lee | Labourer |

Married in the Parish Church according to the Rites and Ceremonies of the Established Church, by me,

This Marriage was solemnized between us: The mark X of Henry Foster, Elizabeth Lee — In the Presence of us: Alfred Foster, John Millburne

MXA 453647

Marriage certificate

Elizabeth was diminutive in stature but big of heart, a determined character who was willing to take on any challenge. She assisted Henry with the farming and cared for the ducks and geese.

Hoping to raise a family and be able to support them and his wife, Henry realized that he would never be able to prosper and would probably have to endure a life of poverty. In the nineteenth century up to fifty percent of farm workers in Buckinghamshire were to leave the farms and get work elsewhere at the time of the Industrial Revolution. Many went to the bigger cities and worked in factories. This was not Henry's wish. At the time there was a famine as well as cholera and typhoid epidemics in the district. He made the decision to immigrate to Australia.

Henry and Elizabeth Foster

Within six weeks after their marriage, Henry and Elizabeth boarded the
Phoebe mastered by Captain William Dale at London and set sail via

Plymouth for Australia. Their exact destination was South Australia, the new colony that was a free colony where one was encouraged to own land and farm it for their own benefit and not for someone else's benefit. Henry's uncle John Foster, accompanied by his wife and family, had immigrated to South Australia in the previous year on the same ship. (Henry's brothers Alfred and David were also to immigrate to South Australia, arriving in the same year as Henry. Henry's other brother Amos later immigrated to South Australia in 1849. Elizabeth's parents William and Elizabeth with their two daughters Jemima and Mary also immigrated to South Australia in 1848.)

An account is hereby given of the conditions which immigrants faced on a typical voyage to the colonies of Australia.

A voyage generally took about three months, usually a perilous one in unseaworthy vessels. The ships were always overcrowded, with cramped conditions, often ill-equipped, continually damp and uncomfortable for passengers. There were hardships for the passengers to face. It generally was a harrowing experience.

If the immigrants were applying for an assisted passage, the applicants had to give evidence that they were sober, honest, hardworking, healthy, industrious and of good moral character. Prior to embarking, the passengers were divided into family groups with up to twelve adults, who would sit together for their meals during the voyage. The reason for this was to establish a collective group of relatives and friends (or even strangers), who could make acquaintances, socialize and then act as a support for each other during the voyage, or even prior to the voyage commencement.

Only the wealthy could afford a cabin, so most passengers were accommodated below decks (below the waterline), in the steerage section of the ship. Passengers in steerage were allowed to take up to twenty cubic feet of luggage, however only one of the permissible two bags was allowed to be kept in their sleeping berth. Married couples with children under twelve shared a partitioned double level bunk which was less than six feet by three feet in space. Those family groups separated the single men located in the bow from the single women located in the stern. (Enclosed cabins accommodated up to seven single females and up to seven single men.) Their separate locations positioned well apart ensured the virtue and morality of the young people. The single men were not permitted to mix with the single women – likewise the single women were not allowed to fraternize with the single men or the crew. Rules however were made to be broken.

The ship had a school which was provided for the children on board. There was a hospital with separate areas for men and women. The toilet for women and children was below decks. (The men had to go up onto deck to the leeward side of the ship.) There was an oven for making bread and clotheslines for drying clothes. It was not possible to wash heavy clothing on the voyage, only small things, due to the limited fresh water available.

A group committee was elected by the passengers from among themselves. The committee was to ensure that order was preserved, the decks kept clean and the proper allowance and correct type of provisions issued. A new committee had to be elected at the end of each month.

There was also a matron's committee comprising of six females of mature age who watched over the young females and ensured that they were in their sleeping apartments at the proper hour, subsequently not being tempted to break the fraternization rules. The matrons did not retire themselves until the maidens were safe in their own beds.

During storms the hatches were frequently closed to prevent seawater and often torrential rain flushing through the living quarters. Seasickness was prevalent among the passengers as the ship pitched violently and relentlessly during high seas giving no respite. Small portholes were closed to keep out the spray, causing the air to become putrid with the stench of illness and vomit.

In the tropics the conditions were oppressive, and the heat was unbearable, being combined with the high humidity. Very few if any of the passengers had previously experienced that kind of weather. When the ship was becalmed for days without a whisper of breeze, boredom for the passengers was the result. Their continual scanning of the horizon never seemed to achieve a sighting of land, although sea creatures such as dolphins, sharks, whales, giant squid and the occasional albatross did arouse their curiosity. A few passengers tried their hand at fishing, endeavouring to supplement their meagre diet.

There were activities for the amusement of the passengers such as music, singing and concerts which were a welcome diversion. Card playing, gambling and drunkenness often led to squabbles, fights and general trouble, so were prohibited. Sunday was a time for church services. When attending, passengers were expected to clean up their appearance as well as their behaviour and morals.

The Captain was in charge of the crew. The Surgeon Superintendent had the responsibility for the welfare of the passengers. (He had the special privilege of sitting at the Captain's table for each meal.) He was in control of health, nutrition, conduct, morals and often gave spiritual guidance.

It was common for many passengers, particularly children, not to survive the voyage. After a short religious service, the bodies were thrown overboard. The ships were referred to as "coffin ships" as on occasions up to ten percent of the passengers did not survive the voyage. It was also common for several births to occur at sea. The Surgeon Superintendent was paid an extra bonus for each child born, but at the same time a deduction was made from his wage for every death on the voyage.

The passengers were given a health check before departure; many illnesses and diseases however were not detected. Many died during the voyage from typhoid, cholera, tuberculosis, scarlet fever, diarrhoea and complications from measles and whooping cough. Poor diet, the damp conditions, stale air in confined areas and the lack of cleanliness encouraged illness which once established spread quickly through the ship. The newborn babies often did not survive in the unsanitary conditions.

Food for the passengers was in limited supply, consisting of small amounts of bread, salted meat, stews, pickled fish, soup, suet, oatmeal and puddings.

Weevils and rats on the ship enjoyed the food more than the passengers. Men and women received equal shares of food, however children aged under 14 years received only a half share of rations. Medical supplies were issued by the Surgeon Superintendent (at his whim) to passengers. They included arrowroot, sugar, sage, lime and lemon juice and bottles of wine, port, stout and rum.

Emigrants on deck

Some extracts from the 'Rules for immigrant ships – Passenger Act 1847' from John Capper's *the Emigrant's Guide to Australia 1853* are listed:

- Every passenger to rise at 7 a.m. unless otherwise permitted by the surgeon, or, if no surgeon, the master.
- Breakfast from 8 till 9 a.m. dinner at 1 p.m. and supper at 6 p.m.
- The passengers to be in their beds by 10 p.m.
- Fires to be lit by the passenger's cook and kept alight till 7 p.m. then to be extinguished, unless otherwise directed by the master or required for use of the sick.
- The master to determine the order in which the passengers shall be entitled to the use of the fires for cooking. The cook to take care that this order is preserved.
- Three safety lights to be lit at dusk, one to be kept burning all night in the main hatchway, the two others may be extinguished by 10 p.m.
- No naked light to be allowed at any time or on any account.
- Passengers when dressed, to roll up their beds, to sweep the decks (including the space under the bottom of the berths), and to throw the dirt overboard.
- Breakfast not to commence until this is done
- The sweepers for the day to be taken in rotation from the males above 14, in the proportion of five for every one hundred passengers.

- Duties of the sweepers to be to clean the ladders, hospital, round-houses, to sweep the decks after every meal and to dry holystone and scrape them after breakfast.

- The occupant of each berth to see that his own is well brushed out and single women are to keep their own compartment clean in ships where a separate compartment is allotted to them.

- The beds to be well shaken and aired on deck and the bottom boards, if not fixtures, to be removed and dry-scrubbed and taken on deck at least twice a week.

- Two days in the week to be appointed by the master as washing days, but no clothes to be washed or dried between decks.

- The coppers and cooking vessels to be cleaned every day.

- The scuttles and stern ports, if any, to be kept open (weather permitting) from 7 a.m. to 10 p.m. and the hatches at all hours.

- Hospitals to be established, with an area, in ships carrying one hundred passengers, of not less than forty-eight superficial feet, with two or four bed berths; and in ships carrying two hundred passengers, of not less than one hundred superficial feet, with six bed-berths.

- On Sunday the passengers to be mustered at 10 a.m. when they will be expected to appear in clean and decent apparel. The day to be observed as religiously as circumstances will permit.

- No spirits or gunpowder to be taken on board by any passenger. Any that may be discovered to be taken into custody of the master till the expiration of the voyage.
- No loose hay or straw to be allowed below.
- No smoking allowed between decks.
- Passengers must leave the poop deck by 8-30 p.m. to be in beds by 10 p.m.
- All gambling, fighting, riotous or quarrelsome behaviour, swearing and violent language to be at once put a stop to. Swords and other offensive weapons, as soon as the passengers embark, to be placed in the custody of the master.
- No sailors to remain on the passenger deck among the passengers except on duty.
- No passenger to go to the ship's cookhouse without special permission from the master, nor to remain in the forecastle among the sailors on any account.
- Passengers advised to bring with them tea, sugar, treacle, cheese and herrings. Raspberry wine or vinegar useful for adding to drinking water. Utensils such as knife, fork, spoon, metal plate, mug to be given to passengers, can be kept by those who have behaved well on the voyage.

The Foster family survived their voyage to Australia and kept their utensils. The Phoebe arrived at Port Adelaide in early 1847 after a voyage lasting 95 days, with 230 immigrants aboard. The number had been increased by one on the voyage as Elizabeth gave birth to a son, Edwin, while at sea. Sadly, their son was to die after living less than a month in the Colony after their arrival.

Henry and Elizabeth were devastated by the death of their newly born. The immediate response was that Elizabeth wanted to return home to the comfort of family and friends. Her distressed feeling was much more than just homesickness. They reviewed their situation. Henry's uncle was already in the Colony, his two brothers were already on their way to South Australia, a third brother was planning to immigrate in a year or two, and most importantly for Elizabeth, her parents and two sisters were intending to immigrate to South Australia in the following year. In a short period of time the family would be together again. They decided to stay.

Work was found initially by Henry as a sawyer in the Adelaide Hills in an area called New Tiers (near present day Crafers). The hills were thickly wooded with large eucalypt trees including stringy bark, blue gum and river red gum. Those who had already bought allotments of land required assistance from willing workers to fell many of the trees to enable the land to be cleared for farming. Working as a sawyer was extremely hard manual work, using an axe and a saw, without any sophisticated machinery available. Henry also worked as an agricultural labourer in Kensington and Magill.

Henry was again working as an agricultural labourer for someone else. (Three children were born during this time.) After seven years of extremely hard work however, he had saved enough money to be able to put a deposit on 104 acres of land in section 943 of Brownhill Creek. Once again, Henry was busy felling trees and clearing scrub to enable land to be used for farming, a mammoth job as it was thickly wooded and some areas were steeply inclined. This time however he was working for himself on his own land.

Three years later Henry took out a mortgage to build a house on the property. (Two more children had been born at that stage.) The house Henry built was called "Lilydale" and became the family home for the Fosters in Australia. (Prior to building the house, Henry and Elizabeth with their small children would have endeavoured to survive while living in a basic bark hut, not dissimilar to the wurlies that the aborigines lived in.)

Lilydale was located in quite an isolated spot. After land around the house was cleared by a lot of backbreaking work, Henry was able to successfully grow spring vegetables as well as plant some fruit trees. The pear trees particularly were to become prolific with fruit. Although the soil became dry in the summer months, it did not need as much watering as some other areas in the district did.

Bushfires (or the threat of) were a constant danger and concern. (In 1951 three policemen were lost in a bushfire at Foster's Gully, at a gully on Henry's original property. A plaque commemorating the loss is still there.) Extreme heat, bitter cold and floods were always not far away. Drought was the major fear of most settlers, however the elevated position of Henry's property in the Adelaide Hills meant that there was rain falling in the hills more often than on the plains.

Bushfire plaque

By 1870, a further four children had been born. Henry purchased additional land from Peter Prankard and William Galbraith, being allotments 940, 941 and 976, a total of 264 acres on the upper reaches (southern side) of Brownhill Creek. Henry set about to expand his market garden and build a "mini empire," with three strong sons to help. He fed them heaps of vegetables and gave them heaps of hard work. They grew potatoes, cabbages, beans, peas, carrots, celery, onions, beetroot, parsnips and turnips. They also had several fruit trees. The business thrived. This was what Henry had dreamed of. Not working for the squire in Buckinghamshire, but working for himself, the profits benefiting his own growing family

Brownhill Creek

Brownhill Creek was originally known as Wirraparinga by the Kaurna aboriginal tribe, which had hunted there. The word means "scrubby place by water."

Brownhill Creek was surveyed in 1838. Initially the South Australian Company ran a sheep station there, but after a short time it was abandoned. The fertile peaty alluvial soils of the creek flats, accompanied by generally good climatic conditions, resulted in the area being suitable for market gardening. The area had to be cleared of trees and undergrowth. Bullock teams hauled the felled trees along rough and slippery tracks and often had to negotiate steep tracks which were very dangerous when wet.

Seasonally the winter frosts were not a major problem and in the hot summer there was generally limited water from the creek to be used for irrigation. The creek had its start in the Crafers area and meandered in a north-westerly direction on to the Adelaide Plains towards the coast. Mitcham Village was the nearest settlement. The second hotel to open there in 1852 was named the "Brownhill Creek Inn." The city of Adelaide could be reached from Brownhill Creek in less than a day in travel; subsequently the market gardeners could regularly sell their produce to a large and stable market.

Brownhill Creek market gardens

For the settlers in Brownhill Creek there was a living to be made if they were willing to work. The lifestyle was simple but idyllic. The children grew up in a safe and natural environment. They swam in the creek, exercised by climbing up and down hills, tended to the animals, picked wildflowers, blackberries and mushrooms, caught tadpoles in the creek and chased butterflies in the cotton bushes. They were also on hand to assist with the market gardening activities when required.

Brownhill Creek produce

Brownhill Creek was a very close-knit, isolated community with many families only ever seeing members of neighbouring families, as there weren't any travellers "passing through" or many visitors from other locations. Everyone knew everyone and socializing was done at the local Baptist Church which had been built in 1874. (It also later served as the Brownhill Creek local school.) Families were large – Henry had eight surviving children. (At Brownhill Creek his son Edwin was to later have sixteen children where another son Albert was to later have thirteen children.)

Edwin (Ted) Foster

It was only natural that the families of Brownhill Creek intermarried. Apart from everyone knowing each other, everyone was related to each other! The Fosters married into family names such as Grimes, Mitchell, Slater, Frisby, Hodge, Craker, Tilley and Rogers – all were known names in the area. With families as large as sixteen children, the Foster name became widespread throughout the district. (My own grandmother Elsey Foster was one of sixteen children.)

After toiling in the market gardens from dawn to dusk each day of the week (apart from Sunday when they were at church), the Brownhill Creek market gardeners looked forward to the day when they took their fruit and vegetable produce in their horse-drawn wagons to the East End Market in Adelaide. They would leave at 4-00 a.m. – up to three times per week. They were able to rest their weary limbs and let the horses pull the wagons, a welcome respite from the back-breaking work of gardening each day.

After selling their produce at the market, they would collect animal manure in their empty wagons from stables in Adelaide to use as fertilizer for the market gardens. On the return journey, at Brownhill Creek it was necessary to dump part of the manure load to enable the horses to pull their heavy load up the steep hills. This manure started to pollute the creek, and after some complaints from locals, the market gardeners built concrete manure holding pits, (which still exist to this day).

Visiting Adelaide was an opportunity for them to meet neighbours, to socialize with friends (and relatives) as they travelled in convoy. It also was a time, if they were so inclined, to visit one of the public houses for a drink or two or three. The market gardeners would sell their products and, with money in their pockets, be faced with a decision to make – whether or not they should be tempted and imbibe.

If they fell to the temptation the horses knew the way home. Upon arrival at home the horses would wait patiently, still harnessed, by the house until the irate wife would come out to unhitch them from the cart. At the same time the wife would vehemently be saying some very meaningful words to her beloved husband. (Whether he heard them or not depended on the state he was in!)

In the nearby German settlement town of Hahndorf, in those early days it was a different situation. The women would walk through the foothills, taking their fresh produce to the market in Adelaide. (They would return carrying house bricks in their sacks to be put towards building the new Lutheran church). Hahndorf was a much more accessible place than the sheltered and isolated Brownhill Creek. Regrettably some of the German women were molested on their walk by escaped convicts, bushrangers or any others who may have had sinister intentions. To solve this problem the Hahndorf *Frauen* and *Fraulein*, (wielding sticks for protection), walked to the market through the night under the cover of darkness to hopefully avoid any such confrontations.

In 1879, Henry leased out land in section 941 to John Brooks who wanted to quarry stone. The quarrymen commenced work and the Foster children were entertained and amused to watch the workmen cart stone from the quarry. The men were loudly swearing as they urged the horses to pull the five-horse carts along the slippery, muddy tracks. It was an education that the children were not receiving at Sunday School.

Foster's Bend

Further land was transferred by Henry to Arthur Blyth to accommodate the new railway line to Bridgewater. The Adelaide to Melbourne express was to eventually to travel this line and the bend where the land had been acquisitioned is still known as Foster's Bend. The locals had coined the name for the general area as "Fosterville."

Henry was to pay off his original mortgage in 1880. His intention was to build a substantial house on his new land, a house which all his family could gather in and enjoy. He chose to build a freestone house with veranda in a prominent position on Sheoak Road. (It was later used as a horse-riding school known as the Sheoak Hill Riding School.)

Henry called it "The Big House." Later however it was to be called "Foster's Folly" by the locals, as once it had been built all of Henry's children married and moved out to raise their own families, leaving Henry and Elizabeth alone in the large multi-roomed house. This situation was to change after Henry's death. (See later.)

Fosterville, the "Big House"

At times Henry was occasionally involved in situations with the police and the authorities. On one occasion he was brought to court for seizing stray sheep which were on his property and taking them to the pound. His son Edwin, as a witness, said that the sheep had strayed onto their property. Two shepherds were nearby. When asked as to who the sheep belonged to, they refused to answer and threatened to kill Edwin. The sheep were duly taken to the local pound until the owner could be found. Henry went to the city to see his solicitor. His son Albert was also a witness at the court. He gave corroborative evidence. The magistrate told the jury that they had to decide if (a) the sheep had been seized legally, and (b) the sheep were taken to the nearest pound with due care. The jury found in favour of the defendant on each point.

In 1883 Henry was a witness at an enquiry with the coroner regarding a series of fires that had been set in the district. There had been five acts of arson over a four-year period, including one which burnt Henry's property and came within 200 yards of his house. Another of these fires had burnt down the stables belonging to Henry's son Albert. A culprit was eventually captured – a local who held a grievance against a neighbour who had reported him to the police regarding acts of bestiality. In vengeance he had committed the acts of arson.

As often happened in pioneering communities in those early days, tragedies occurred. Henry Foster was not exempt from experiencing them within his own extended family. Many sad incidents occurred during his lifetime and even after his death.

Henry and Elizabeth in the early days of their marriage had the heart-breaking loss of their first son, born at sea on the Phoebe. He died shortly after arriving in South Australia. It must have been a devastating blow for them at the time, being half a world away from their family and friends in England.

Another Foster relative and his wife had a heart-breaking time in raising children. Of their six children, five were to die as toddlers. A tragic situation for parents raising a young family, almost beyond belief. (Amazingly their sixth and only surviving child lived to be ninety!)

Henry's son Arthur suffered the loss of his wife Charlotte, only one day after the death of their 15 days old son. Arthur, a teamster, was Henry's second son. He himself was killed when his trolley pulled by four horses was hit by the Melbourne-to-Adelaide express train at the Cross Road Unley Park level railway crossing.

Arthur had been to Clovelly Park to collect a load of manure for his market garden. The engine driver of the Melbourne Express had sounded the whistle and applied the brakes as it approached the crossing, however Arthur had attempted to cross in front of the train. He had whipped the horses but failed to cross the line in time. Two of the horses were killed instantly and a third had to be put down due to its injuries. Arthur was thrown ten feet clear of the line and received serious injuries, although was conscious after the accident. The warning gong at the crossing had been operating. He was transported by the same train to Adelaide and then by cart to the Royal Adelaide Hospital. He had compound fractures of both legs and a hip, two fractures to the skull, plus severe cuts and bruises to his head and body. On the next day, he died of shock from his injuries.

At an inquest held the following week by the acting City Coroner, it was stated that Henry Foster junior (Arthur's brother) had identified the body. Remarkably a witness claimed that he had seen the same driver and same cart attempt the same crossing two years earlier. On that occasion the train managed to stop ten feet before the crossing. (Arthur had been known to have had other accidents in his horse and cart, on one occasion breaking his arm.) Another witness stated that Foster, when still conscious, had confirmed to him that he had been aware of the train and had tried to pass in front of it. The jury returned a verdict of accidental death and in their opinion no blame could be attached to anyone else but the victim.

Family folklore suggests that Arthur may have been drinking at a pub prior to the accident. However, as the accident happened before 9-00 a.m. and he had already collected his load of manure that morning, this suggestion seems highly unlikely.

There were also other tragedies. Henry's grandson Herbert Foster was burnt to death at Brownhill Creek when playing with matches. He set fire to surrounding dry grass and subsequently his clothes and himself. He died two hours later. Herbert was only two years and five months of age.

In another incident, in Melbourne, Henry's granddaughter Esther was murdered (by gunshot) by her husband Jeret Fondaberry (who then committed suicide). Esther had been having an affair with another man.

Possibly the most tragic event of all happened to another of the Foster young grandsons. He was playing "hide and seek" with his older sister at home. He ran off to hide while his sister counted and then gave the call "coming ready or not." She searched and searched but could not find him. Her parents then joined in the search. About an hour later his body was found at the bottom of the well. He had climbed into the well to hide – and had fallen to his death. He was only three years of age.

Brownhill Creek market gardeners were well represented on the honour board at the Brownhill Creek chapel/school for those who fought in World War I. Of the eighteen names listed on the honour board for Brownhill Creek, four were Fosters. William Charles Foster and John Ernest Foster (both grandsons of Henry Foster) were killed in action in France in World War I.

Henry Foster was to die in 1889 at Belair of heart exhaustion, pneumonia and senile decay. He was buried at the Mitcham Cemetery Church of England section. The inscription on his tombstone read:

> His days were numbered: he is gone,
> From all these earthly things,
> Hoping to find eternal rest,
> With Christ the king of kings.

In his will Henry left his property to his wife Elizabeth. Each daughter received 150 pounds and each son a share of his property upon Elizabeth's demise. The executors were George Craker and Henry's son Albert. Henry had signed his will with an 'X'.

Upon Henry's death Elizabeth was left alone in the "Big House." It was decided that her son Edwin, (who was to eventually have sixteen children), would occupy the property. Elizabeth spent time with Edwin but also spent time at the homes of her other children. Edwin had married Ellen Slater, who was the daughter of Dutchman John Slater (previously known as Tjitse van der Leij). Edwin's brother Albert had married Eliza Slater, another daughter of John Slater. They were to have thirteen children. There was some jealousy and animosity between the two sisters. Eliza resented the fact that Ellen lived in the "Big House" with her large family, when she had to live in a lesser dwelling with her many children. She considered her sister to be "well off," whereas she classified herself as "poor."

Elizabeth Foster was to die of senile decay in 1915 at the Mitcham home of her daughter Harriet. Although depicted as a diminutive and petite woman in photos, she reached the grand age of 88 years. When she met Henry, she was a young woman who helped look after his ducks and geese. When she died it was reported that she left 7 children, 67 grandchildren, 74 great grandchildren and 3 great great grandchildren making a total of 151 living descendants. She was buried alongside her husband Henry at the Church of England section of the Mitcham Cemetery.

In 1918, a public auction was held for Henry's estate. 158 acres and three houses were sold for 1300 pounds, and 104 acres and a quarry were sold for 750 pounds. Many of his descendants continued to live and work in the Brownhill Creek area. Henry Foster had from 1854 established a business in Brownhill Creek and he and his descendants successfully worked the market gardens in that district for a total period of 112 years.

Henry Foster tombstone

The author at Foster's Hill

Conclusion:

HENRY FOSTER (1821 – 1889)

Just a name and a date? Research has shown that Henry was born into a farming community in Buckinghamshire, England, into a system of working as an agricultural labourer for a squire, just as his father and earlier generations had. This was the hand he had been dealt.

Why did he come to Australia?  Working long hours for a meagre wage, after marriage he could see his future was limited, so he had the foresight and courage to immigrate with his newly wedded wife Elizabeth to South Australia. It was possible there to own land, not just work on someone else's land for their benefit.

In Australia he started from scratch, engaging in back-breaking work to at last be able to buy his own land and farm it. This was Henry's dream. He never ever faltered from the course of achieving this aim. He overcame the adversity of bushfires, floods, droughts and crop diseases. After having worked for a squire in England, he eventually became unofficially known as the "Squire of Brownhill Creek." In the district, Foster's Gully, Foster's Hill, Foster's Bend and Fosterville were named after him. Henry had become a most respected member of the local market gardening community.

Henry and his wife raised their children with the principles of love of family, hard work and sound morals. They overcame various setbacks including loss of family members, yet still determinedly carried on. They produced a multitude of Fosters to thrive throughout the Adelaide Hills (providing they followed Henry's example of honest hard work). When Elizabeth died, she left behind 151 descendants – Henry and Elizabeth certainly had contributed to boosting Australia's population!

In photographs Henry appeared to be a man of average build with plastered down parted hair and some whiskers. His weathered face gave the impression of a strong determined man who knew what he wanted to achieve in life (and perhaps had reached that goal).

Henry died in 1889. He had signed his marriage certificate with an 'X'. Near the end of his life he signed his will with an 'X'. A great lifetime achievement by (in some ways) an uneducated man, to become a successful market gardener, farm manager, husband, father and prominent pioneer.

He was my great great grandfather.

Weavers' houses at Bethnal Green

# 2

# WILLIAM DEARING

## 1835 – 1914

# FAMILY TREE

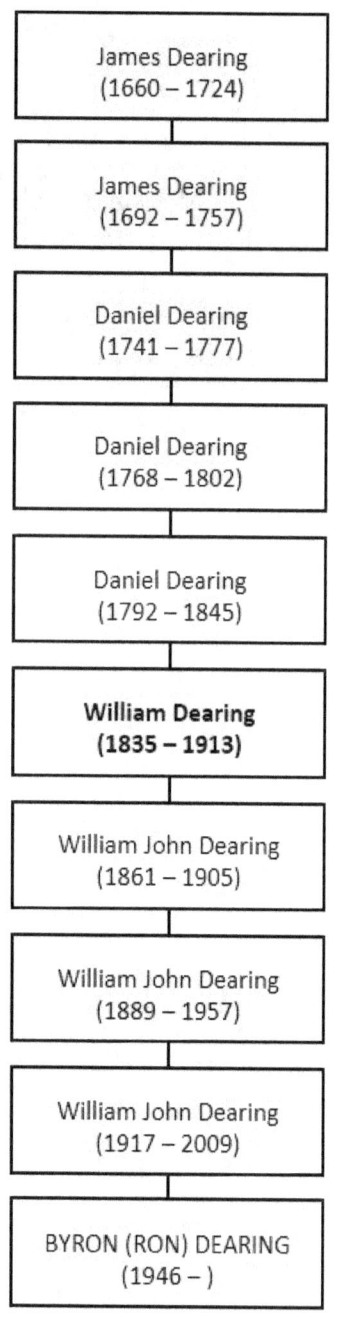

James Dearing
(1660 – 1724)

James Dearing
(1692 – 1757)

Daniel Dearing
(1741 – 1777)

Daniel Dearing
(1768 – 1802)

Daniel Dearing
(1792 – 1845)

**William Dearing**
**(1835 – 1913)**

William John Dearing
(1861 – 1905)

William John Dearing
(1889 – 1957)

William John Dearing
(1917 – 2009)

BYRON (RON) DEARING
(1946 – )

The surname Dearing is a form of an old English word meaning "son of the brave, bold or fierce." As there have been multiple spellings of the name over time, it has also been suggested that it could also mean "son of the dear or beloved."

As a young boy I had asked my father as to where the Dearings had come from. My father appeared to have little interest or knowledge and answered by just shrugging his shoulders. "It's a mystery," he responded, almost dismissing the question, much to my annoyance. My great uncle "Uncle Fred" however was quite specific when asked the same question. He adamantly claimed that the Dearings were German. "William Dearing was Wilhelm Doering" he insisted. It was not until I began researching my family tree that I discovered that my great grandfather's wedding certificate stated he had been born in London. The Dearings were English. So much for Uncle Fred's German theory!

The Dearing family of East London, England have been traced back to the 1600s. (It has been suggested that William the Conqueror offered the Dearings lands in Kent after their assistance to him in the Battle of Hastings in 1066, however this fact is difficult to connect to "my" Dearings of East London.) Beginning with James Dearing (1660 - 1724), there were five successive generations of Dearing silk weavers in the East London area, the fathers having each passed the trade on to their sons.

East London had also been occupied by French Huguenots (Protestants), who had fled France because of religious persecution in the seventeenth and eighteenth centuries. Under the Edict of Nantes in 1598 they had the freedom to worship as they wished, however that edict was revoked by Louis XIV with the Edict of Fontainebleau in 1685 and the Huguenots were forced to become Roman Catholics, or alternatively flee the country to avoid imprisonment. Many French Huguenots had fled France and had come to East London as refugees. Many were silk weavers and brought their skills and trade with them. My five times great grandfather Daniel Dearing was to marry a French Huguenot in 1765 and his son Daniel (my four times great grandfather) was also to marry a French Huguenot in 1791. Subsequently we Dearings do have some French blood flowing in our veins.

William Dearing was born in 1835 at Bethnal Green in the Bethnal Green workhouse to Daniel Dearing and Charlotte Read. His father was a silk weaver, having been taught the trade by his father. His grandmother Ann (née Fra) had also worked as a silk weaver as did his great grandmother Jane (née Heck). They were both French Huguenots. William was the second youngest of five sons. The fact that William had been born in the notorious workhouse indicated that life was not going well for the Dearing family, as being in a workhouse was akin to being on the bottom rung of the social ladder.

In the early eighteenth-century, Bethnal Green, where William was born, was in the parish of Stepney. It was a small hamlet of pleasant countryside and marshy forest with some fertile farming land. Being outside the city walls of London, Royalty would often come to the area of open spaces for hunting expeditions.

It was originally called Blithehole or Blythhole, which loosely meant "Happy Corner." On the old Roman Road, a large mansion was built in 1570, called Bednall House, later to be called Kirby's Castle. (This was to be turned into a mental asylum, eventually being demolished in 1843.) The park where it stood was (and still is) known by locals as "Barmy Park."

The eighteenth century saw increased settlement as the influx of silk weavers, including ones from France as well as Ireland, came to Bethnal Green. Initially they had been operating their looms in Spitafields and Mile End Town, however the overcrowding caused a spill-over to the Bethnal Green area. In 1743, Bethnal Green had separated from the Stepney parish and had become its own locale.

The movement of silk weavers to Bethnal Green continued into the nineteenth century, with the silk weaving becoming a flourishing industry. Bethnal Green had become a place including immigrants of many different nationalities. There were street vendors, food sellers, entertainers, musicians, dog and bird fanciers. There were also pick pockets, prostitutes, shop lifters, beggars, tramps, dog stealers and cock fighting entrepreneurs, all of whom called for a continual police presence in the district.

Being born in East London means that most of the Dearings could be considered Cockneys. Traditionally, one was considered to be a Cockney if born within the sound of the Bow Bells of St. Mary-le-Bow Church at Cheapside, London. It would depend on how strong the wind was and from what direction the wind was blowing at the time of birth. The quality of the listener's hearing would have to be taken into consideration.

St Mary-le-Bow church

The Dearings would have been familiar with the Cockney rhyming slang used. For example: "Plates of meat" were feet. "Butcher's hook" was look. "Trouble and strife" were wife. "Daisy roots" were boots, etc. This type of secret code was initially used by the Cockneys when being interrogated by the constabulary or authorities. They were able to converse with each other without the interrogator understanding the meanings.

The situation for the Bethnal Green silk weavers however was to become dire, as described in the diary of Charles Greville in 1832:

A man came yesterday from Bethnal Green with an account of that district. They are all weavers, forming a separate community, there they are born, there they live and labour, and there they die. They neither migrate nor change their occupation. They can do nothing else. They have increased in a ratio at variance with any principles of population, having nearly tripled in twenty years from 22,000 to 62,000. They are for the most part out of employment and can get none. 1,100 are crammed into the poor house, five or six in a bed. 6,000 receive parochial relief. The parish is in debt, every day adds to the number of paupers and diminishes that of the ratepayers. These are principally small shopkeepers, who are beggared by the rates. The district is in a complete state of insolvency and hopeless poverty, yet they multiply, and while the people look squalid and dejected, as if borne down by their wretchedness and destitution, the children seem happy. Government is ready to interpose with assistance, but what can Government do? We asked the man who came what could be done for them. He said "employment," and employment is impossible.

William's father Daniel was to die in the workhouse in 1845. A newspaper reported at the time that Daniel had been upset that he feared that one of his sons may be transported to Australia and he would be unable to visit him in jail prior to the transportation. William's mother Charlotte was also regularly in and out of the workhouse, her father also having died in the workhouse.

Dinner time at the workhouse

The notorious workhouses in England were a public institution where people who were unable to support themselves were housed and (if able-bodied) made to work. It was often the final abode, or only abode for many of the residents. Charles Dickens often wrote about the dreaded workhouses, as he aptly depicted in his book *Oliver Twist*, the main character being born in a workhouse. The Lancet Medical Journal of the time reported realistically on the terrible conditions faced by the inmates in the Bethnal Green workhouse:

- No running water was available from 5 p.m. until 7 a.m.

- Classification was poor, with imbeciles scattered among various wards and foul cases mixed with ordinary patients.

- Lighting and ventilation were inadequate – many windows were six feet from the floor to prevent inmates from seeing out.

- Overcrowding resulted in each patient having only 300 cubic foot, only a quarter of the official recommendations.

- There was a lack of water closets and floors were soaked with urine.

- Washing facilities were severely lacking – in one children's ward seventeen children were washed daily in the one pail, several in the same water, and dried with sheets.

- In the male wards, 45 men were served by two latrines which were flushed twice a day.

- A staff of only two paid nurses, both untrained, nursed up to 600 sick. They were assisted by 40 pauper nurses and helpers "whose tendencies to drink cannot be controlled."

- The insane ward consisted of small, dark, ill-ventilated rooms, under the charge of a male pauper, a weaver by trade with no knowledge of nursing.

- The diet was lacking in meat and the aged and infirmed were given difficult to digest food such as suet pudding.

- The number of medical officers was inadequate for the number of patients.

In the 1851 census William Dearing was shown to be living with his recently married cousin Alfred Mapp at Haggerstone East. (Alfred's mother Elizabeth (née Dearing) Mapp was William's aunt.) William's father Daniel had died six years earlier and his mother Charlotte was alternately spending time with her own family and being in the workhouse. It was a case where William at aged 16 had to fare for himself. His occupation was shown as a cordwainer, someone who works with leather and makes leather goods. The break from the family tradition of being a silk weaver had been caused by the ominous situation of the silk weaving industry being in disarray and heading towards collapse. The individual silk weavers were still using single looms at home, which had been replaced by large automatic looms in factories (part of the Industrial Revolution). As a result, the silk weaving industry in London's East End was doomed. William had made a sensible decision not to follow the Dearing family tradition as a silk weaver. He was eventually to become a bootmaker.

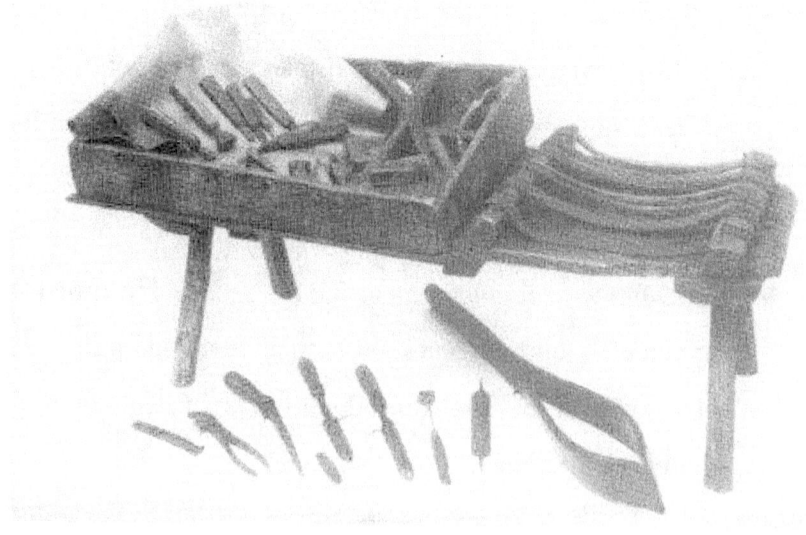

A bootmaker's tools

A weaver at work

An interview with a local:

"Excuse me, sir. I work for a newspaper in Fleet Street and my governor has asked me to come to Bethnal Green to interview a typical local resident."

"If a typical local resident means someone who is looking for work, hungry, bloody cold, trying to avoid catching the epidemics and has sore "plates of meat" – I suppose that would be me."

"What's your name?"

"William Dearing – call me Will."

"How is it spelt?"

"Don't know – never did much schooling."

"How old are you then?"

"Not sure – I was baptized at St. Matthew's in 1835 when King William was on the throne."

"Where did your family come from?"

"We've always been local. The Dearings have been well known in Bethnal Green for years and have relatives all over East London."

"What did your father do?'

"My old man was a weaver as was Grandad and his Dad again. The weaving industry however is almost dead, particularly now that the Government are talking about doing a trade agreement with France for those cheap imports."

"What do you do?"

"My brother John and I have worked as cordwainers. My uncle John offered me work as an undertaker, but I don't fancy that work much. My brother Henry has done well as a bootmaker. Perhaps I can continue that trade of making "daisy roots" for a living. I might well do that. There's no future in weaving."

"Was your father affected by the downturn of the weaving industry?"

"He sure was. He was unemployed and finished up in the Bethnal Green workhouse. He died there. Half my relatives have finished up in the workhouse. My dear old Mum will probably finish up there too. No way do I want to die in a workhouse."

"Do the authorities help at all?"

"The government up in Westminster don't care about us – bloody toffs. You only have to take a "butcher's hook" to see the overflowing open sewers around here and sniff the air to smell the stench. The "Old Bill" is on to everyone here. If you nick a loaf of bread 'cause you are hungry, they send you to the Old Bailey where the "Barnaby Rudge" will send you on a holiday to the colonies for seven years. It happened to a couple of my friends."

"Do you have any plans for the future?"

"I plan to marry my sweetheart Maria. She's a tailoress. St. Matthew's was damaged by the big fire. Maria's sister Elizabeth says we should be able to get married at St. Dunstan's at Stepney. Maria and I hope to have a family, however I don't really want to bring them up in all this."

"Have you ever thought about emigrating?"

"My brother Harry is out in Australia now, even talking about settling in New Zealand. My brother John wants to go. Yes. Maria and I might just consider it."

"Fares can be expensive."

"Oh no, mate. You can travel on the ship below decks in steerage. It costs next to nothing … providing you survive the voyage, I suppose."

William, aged 25, was to marry Maria Detrick, aged 28, a tailoress, in 1860 at St. Dunstan's, Stepney. (Witnesses were Maria's sister Elizabeth and her husband Henry Lowry.) Maria was the daughter of Martin and Betsy Detrick. Martin was a sugar baker. However, he had previously worked as a cow keeper, supplying milk in the area. (He had come from somewhere in continental Europe. It is almost impossible to determine from where exactly, given the umpteen ways of spelling his surname – Detrick, Dietrick, Dedrick, Dietrich etc. – as well as the loss of so many records in continental Europe in both World Wars).

St. Dunstan's at Stepney

An article was written by John Hollingshead in *the Morning Post* in 1861:

Spitafields/Bethnal Green area was on the verge of economic collapse. The area had been inundated with silk weavers. In 1824 there were 25,000 looms in the area. In 1831 there were between 14,000 to 17,000 working looms, by 1861 that had dropped to only 8,000. The area had a population of about 100,000 persons, half of which were entirely dependent on the weaving industry. Many one-storied cottages were being erected for weaving families who were employed as out-workers. In 1835 wages were lower by thirty percent than in 1824 and they did not average more than eight or nine shillings a week. Now (1861) they cannot be higher than seven shillings a week on average.

The decline in the silk weaving industry in the area had started in the late 1700s when local regulations meant the same job could be carried out elsewhere at a significantly reduced cost. Materials that once would have originated in the area were now available from Norwich, Paisley and Dublin. A further blow came in the form of illegal imports from France. The vast profits to be made meant that no policing could prevent the flourishing cross channel trade. In 1826 the prohibition was lifted and legitimized the trade. An eighty percent duty was imposed on all silk imports. Perhaps the final double blows came with the advent of steam power and the 1860 trade agreement with France. The market was flooded as a result with fancy lower priced fabrics from both here and abroad which condemned the weavers to almost inescapable poverty.

William and Maria were to have three sons in London. However, to raise them in the grim conditions of the coal-smoke-stained streets of London was very difficult. Unemployment was high, crime was prevalent, the putrid air was filled with smog, the streets were filthy and drinking water polluted, with resultant outbreaks of cholera and typhoid occurring (up to five hundred cases per day). Authorities believed that cholera was spread by bad smells – not realizing that the polluted water they were drinking was the cause. (The drinking water was very unhealthy – it was actually safer to drink beer!) Rickets and scurvy were also prevalent. The population of London had increased from one million to three million over a short period. (At that time London was the world's most populous city.) William was considering immigrating to Australia to make a new start, seeking new opportunities and hopefully a better lifestyle. He did not wish to finish up at the notorious workhouse and die there as his father had done.

The decision was made. William's brothers Henry (Harry) and John had already immigrated to Australia, while Maria's brother Martin and her sister Elizabeth were wanting to immigrate. William could only afford the cheapest fare available – which meant being in the steerage section in the bowels of the ship. In 1866, William Dearing with his wife Maria and young family left London and duly sailed to Australia as immigrants.

The Dearing family arrived in Australia and were then recorded as travelling from Brisbane to Sydney by ship on the Telegraph (which a year later was wrecked when it ran aground). In 1866 William was listed in a census of New South Wales, being shown as an unemployed bootmaker and living at Sydney Place in Sydney. At this time another son was born at

Redfern. Unable to gain regular employment, William took his family to Melbourne and initially lived at Richmond. They then had a further two sons, however sadly one of them died at the age of only five days. It was not uncommon for children to die young, with the lack of immunizations, medicines and quality hospital care available. It was nevertheless a devastating blow for William and Maria. They knew that it could happen to other people but had not expected it to happen to themselves.

The family was to move to different addresses, mainly in Richmond, Fitzroy and Collingwood. These suburbs at the time were poorer, lower working-class areas not dissimilar to Bethnal Green back in East London, although at the time Melbourne only had a population of less than 200,000 compared to that of London having over three million. It may have been that they were comfortable in that type of environment as it was all they had known during their lives in East London, but it may also have been that they could only afford the cheapest rent available. They were eventually to settle long term at Hoddle Street, Collingwood, with William continuing to work at his trade as a bootmaker. They were located quite near Victoria Park, which was the Collingwood Football (Australian Rules) Club's home ground.

As a child I had always wondered why my two uncles in South Australia barracked for Collingwood in the (then) Victorian Football League. Collingwood were considered by other team supporters as "the hated enemy," just as Port Adelaide were considered "the hated enemy" in South Australian football by other teams' supporters. With their grandfather and great grandfather having lived a punt kick from the Collingwood ground, this explained why they supported the Collingwood Magpies. The parents obviously had passed their enthusiasm for the Collingwood Football Club on to their children.

Two of William's siblings had also immigrated to Australia. His younger brother John, also a cordwainer and then bootmaker, married, had one child and lived in Melbourne at Fitzroy. He had immigrated to Melbourne on the Prince of Wales. John was to die at a relatively young age of 45 years and was buried in an unmarked grave at St. Kilda Cemetery.

William's other (elder) brother Henry (known as Harry) could be described as the "black sheep" or "bad egg" of the family. He immigrated to Melbourne (having previously had several brushes with the law in England). He lived at Richmond, then St. Kilda. Harry married and had three children. He then took his family to Greymouth, New Zealand, on the remote west coast of the South Island, where a fourth child was born. Work was available there in the mining operations. The area was a very bleak and isolated settlement, almost an outpost. Established law and order in Greymouth was in its infancy, making living there a somewhat fragile and dangerous situation.

Harry was taken to court for assault of his Irish wife, having beaten her. In the same incident, Harry had run out of brandy in a drinking session with a couple of mates. They had suggested that he "sell his wife" and put a noose around her neck. In the ensuing fight all were injured. Harry was fined five pounds.

Two years later Harry was again in court for assault, throwing a tumbler at his wife's head. She was black and bruised around the face. He was fined five pounds and ordered to keep the peace for three months. Three months and eight days later Harry once again was in court for beating his fiery Irish wife. However, on this occasion the magistrate reprimanded both husband and wife, as he ruled that she had contributed to the fight. Harry was fined one shilling.

An unclaimed letter had been sent by William to his brother Harry in New Zealand, never being collected. Perhaps Harry was too busy fighting or going to get more supplies of brandy! Harry was to die at Greymouth of cardiac failure, gastritis and, not surprisingly, alcoholism.

William and Maria continued living at Collingwood, with William still working at his trade as a bootmaker. They had five surviving sons, who, growing up in the Collingwood area, all had some "adventures" as young men generally do (particularly if living in Collingwood!).

Eldest son William John was to marry Mary Ann Miller Littleton on 8th August (the eight month) 1888 – a very lucky date if you are Chinese! Mary Ann had been born in Collingwood. Her family had originally emigrated from Bristol in England on the ship the Blue Jacket. In Collingwood, William John worked for a time as a caretaker of the Salvation Army Barracks at Wellington Street, Collingwood. They were to move to Adelaide where William John worked as a bootmaker and lived on Torrens Road, Brompton. They had three sons and one daughter. He was to die in 1905 and was buried in an unmarked grave at Northfield Cemetery.

William John Dearing (born 1861)

William's son Henry (also known as Harry) in 1886 was in court at an inquest regarding the fatal shooting of Charles Crane who was Harry's mate. Harry and Charles were in the laundry skylarking, and Harry pointed a gun at Charles, not realizing it was loaded. He pulled the trigger and Charles was shot fatally. It was determined at the inquest that the death was accidental. Harry was later to marry and have four children and worked as a gardener.

William's son Martin married and had seven children. He was however not the best husband and father. His wife took him to court for a divorce as he had deserted her and his children and paid no support. His last words to her were "I'm going to Western Australia." To avoid being located, he promptly went to Queensland and worked as a cane cutter and remained there until his death. His wife was granted the divorce in his absence in Melbourne and she never saw him again.

William's son Daniel was also in trouble with the law. He was a showman and swinging boat assistant. He had thrown a rock at someone in a dispute. The man had fallen to the ground unconscious. Daniel had panicked and fled – as far away as Western Australia as he feared he had killed the man. A warrant was issued for his arrest. Having stayed for two years in "the West," Daniel returned to Melbourne and turned himself in, willing to face the consequences of his deed and accept his punishment.

The thrown rock fortunately had not killed the man and he had recovered. In court Daniel was fined for assault and not imprisoned. The magistrate considered that the two years of a guilty conscience that he had experienced in Western Australia was enough punishment. Daniel was to also move to Adelaide with his wife and raise a family, having two children and living in the Port Adelaide area. His only blemish there was when he was fined in court for stealing a leg of ham (while drunk). He was fined two pounds.

Youngest son John remained in Melbourne, married and had a family with three children. He was a gardener and a labourer. He managed to keep clear of the law and any wrongdoing. It was with this son John that William chose to live with in his later years. (He was the only son who hadn't shot someone, moved interstate, deserted their wife, thrown a rock or stole a leg of ham while drunk!)

There was another occasion where a Dearing and a gun were not a good mix. It concerned William's grandchildren. I had always wondered as a small child why I had never met my great grandmother Mary Ann. She was called by the family as "Nanna." I didn't meet her till I was seven years of age. She was over ninety when I met her, a short woman with a walking stick and long white hair that ran down the length of her back. Why had she been "hidden" from me?

It was not until I researched a newspaper article dated 1910 that I came to understand. It was reported that a small boy aged seven had been shot dead by a playmate aged eleven in a horrific accident at Torrens Road, Brompton. The boy shot dead was Horace Cooper (the young brother of Mary Ann's new second husband). The shooter was Fred Dearing (Mary Ann's youngest son).

Apparently young Fred and Horace had come home from the nearby school for lunch. Fred had found a handgun left under a newspaper on a table. Playfully Fred pointed the gun at Horace and pulled the trigger, not realizing it was loaded. The bullet entered the left nostril of Horace and its trajectory continued into his brain. He was killed instantly.

The handgun had been carelessly left on the table still loaded by Mary Ann's eldest son William John Dearing (my grandfather). He was a commercial traveller who took a gun with him on country trips for protection. He had just returned from a country trip. He had been momentarily distracted and left the room leaving the gun covered with a newspaper. It was decided not to call an inquest as it was not necessary and an eleven years old child could not be charged with shooting a seven years old child. The shooting was considered accidental.

Mary Ann's first husband William John Dearing (William Dearing's son) had died at a relatively young age of 44. Mary Ann had remarried. She was 46 at the time and she married one of her son's (my grandfather who was 21) mates (who was 23). Some of the family may not have approved of the union. Surely it was her prerogative to marry whoever she wished, no matter what the age difference. That was not enough reason anyway to keep me as a child from meeting her.

The newspaper article had answered some questions for me. Perhaps "Nanna" blamed my grandfather for carelessly leaving the loaded gun within reach. Perhaps "Nanna's" new husband (grandpa's mate) blamed him for the loss of his young brother. Perhaps "Nanna" and my grandpa were still not speaking (perhaps the reason why I never met her until I was seven). After the accidental shooting my grandfather left home and joined the Merchant Navy and over several years visited the Far East, Africa and Europe. Perhaps he was not welcome at his mother's home. Perhaps he had wanted to escape from the traumatic situation. A lot of speculation, but over a short number of years Mary Ann had lost a husband, a son had died at 10 months of age and now a stepson had been tragically shot by her own son. A lot for anyone to bear over a short period of time.

Family feuds with ill feeling can continue for a lifetime. In families some "skeletons in the cupboard" are often swept under the carpet and never discussed (as was done in this case). In spite of this, I was glad that I eventually did meet "Nanna." She was to die the following year after our meeting. She was 92.

Maria Dearing had died in 1904 of asthma bronchitis and heart failure at Collingwood and was buried alongside William's brother John at St. Kilda Cemetery in an unmarked grave. After Maria's death, William lived with his son John and his wife Jamesina ("Ina") at Collingwood until 1912. William eventually moved to the Cheltenham Benevolent Asylum as his health was declining and he was no longer able to care for himself or be cared for, as his son John was also in ill health.

Unmarked grave of Maria Dearing at St. Kilda, Victoria

William was listed as an old age pensioner. He was to die in 1913, of heart failure and senile decay. He was buried in an unmarked grave at the Cheltenham Pioneers Cemetery in Victoria.

Footnotes:

The Dearing Family Tree shows a succession of continually occurring names, particularly the eldest son being named after the father. As from 1741 onwards there were three Daniels, then a William, then four William Johns (the last William John being my father). When my elder (first-born) brother was named, he was called Donald William and I, as second-born, was called Byron (Ron) John. Grandpa did not speak to Dad for a month as Dad had broken the family tradition of naming the first-born son the same as the father! (My Dad once explained that he did this because mail kept being put in his letter box addressed to his father, who lived next door, which annoyed him.) My brother partly righted the situation as he called his sons Mark William and Stephen John. The situation was further appeased when my son Todd Matthew Dearing changed his name by deed poll to Todd William Dearing, in recognition of his ancestors.

The other unusual aspect of the Dearing Family Tree is that as from 1826 in the direct Dearing line there were 24 males born and only one female. Daniel Dearing (born 1792) had five sons, William (born 1835) had six sons, William John (born 1861) had three sons and one daughter, William John (born 1889) had three sons, William John (born 1917) had two sons, Donald William (born 1942) had two sons and Mark William (born 1966) had three sons. What would be the odds of Mark William's first-born son Mitchell having a daughter?

My Dearing family with myself bottom right on my 4<sup>th</sup> birthday

Conclusion:

WILLIAM DEARING (1835 – 1913)

Just a name and a date? Research has shown that William Dearing was born in a dismal workhouse at Bethnal Green, England, the same workhouse where his father was to die. To be born in the dreaded workhouse was about the worst start William could have in life. Just to survive in growing up in the deplorable conditions of the East London slums would have been a challenge. William would have needed to take care of himself, and be "street smart" as a youth, to avoid any potentially dangerous situations he may encounter.

The Dearing family previously had many generations of weavers, but the silk-weaving industry was in collapse. William managed to learn another trade, rather than be dependent on the silk-weaving industry which his family knew. He eventually became a bootmaker.

Why did he come to Australia? The East End area of London became the worst slums in England as overcrowding, unemployment, abject poverty, open sewers, disease and polluted air and water became widespread. William married Maria and started a family, but with no escape seeming likely from the wretched living conditions, made the wise decision to immigrate to Australia. They left a life of certain poverty behind them. A difficult decision to make, but the impoverished William had the courage to make it, for his family's future benefit.

The family survived the sea voyage to Australia and, after going to Brisbane and Sydney, eventually settled in Melbourne in the poorer parts of the city. William, with his wife, brought up five sons in Collingwood (which was a challenging environment). William fed and raised his family and continued his trade as a bootmaker to support them. There were several other challenges to meet, including his sons having several brushes with law. However, with the support of his wife, he continued on.

His was a hard-fought life, doing what he knew best. His determination, commitment and example created an opportunity for each of his sons and their future generations to grow up in Australia with a more comfortable living, access employment and enjoy a better life.

Maria died and William then slowly succumbed to old age and senility. When he died at the Cheltenham Benevolent Asylum, he was 77 years of age. He was buried in an unmarked grave at the Cheltenham Pioneer Cemetery in suburban Cheltenham in Melbourne.

He was my great great grandfather.

Tjitse van der Leij (John Slater)

# [ 3 ]

# TJITSE RENSE VAN DER LEIJ
# (JOHN SLATER)


**1830 – 1914**

# FAMILY TREE

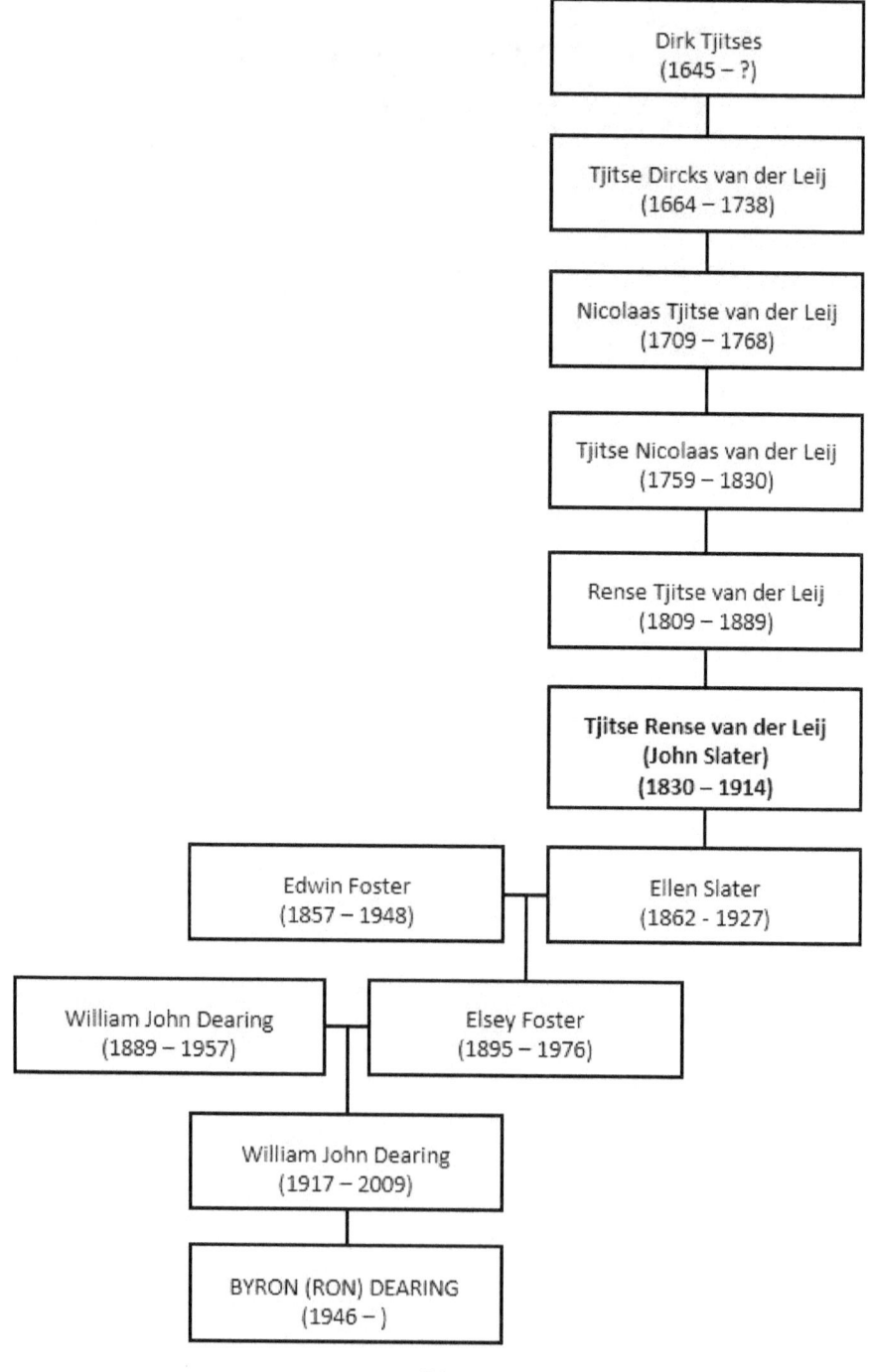

The van der Leij family have been traced back to about 1600, living in Friesland, a northern province of the Netherlands. Those from Friesland were originally a Germanic ethic group and had their own culture and own unique language (Frisian). They were looked upon by other Dutch citizens as a poorer class of people and somewhat "different" (and perhaps still are).

In those early days there were no surnames. The traditional procedure was to name the first-born son after the paternal grandfather, the first-born daughter after the maternal grandmother, the second-born son after the maternal grandfather, the second-born daughter after the paternal grandmother, the third-born son after the father, and the third-born daughter after the mother. Confusion regarding names and family connections was a common occurrence, particularly with so many children born in families.

The great great grandfather of Tjitse Rense van der Leij was Tjitse Dircks (his name before surnames). He lived in the small village of de Leij in Friesland. When in about 1700 he moved to the larger town of Leeuwarden for work (the new town being about fifteen kilometres further south), he became known as Tjitse Dircks "van der Leij" (meaning Tjitse Dircks "of or from the village of Leij"). That family surname subsequently stuck, although the subsequent generations continued to use the traditional method of naming children in order of their birth after their grandparents and parents' Christian names in addition to the surname.

Tjitse Rense van der Leij was born in the town of Gorredijk in the Netherlands in 1830 to Rense van der Leij and Grietje (Margaret) Brandsma, who had married in 1829. Gorredijk was a small village in a farming community and was a market town. The market specialized in quality livestock, fine butter and grains. In Tjitse's time, as well as general farming, there was an industry of excavating peat (vegetable matter decomposed by water in bogs) from the raised bog and transporting it by barges along the canal which ran from Gorredijk to the nearby town of Smilde. The peat was dried, cut into pieces, and used as a fuel to burn or used in horticulture.

Gorredijk, Netherlands

The mother of Tjitse was Grietje (née Brandsma), known as Margaret. According to family folklore, she was a champion ice skater and had been successful in competitions. Tragically in 1831 she died at the age of 24 years (when Tjitse was only six months old), after a heavy fall while skating on the ice. She had been pregnant with her second child at the time. The horrific loss was a devastating blow to her young husband Rense and left her infant only son Tjitse motherless.

The father of Tjitse was Rense. He had been born in Gorredijk, in 1809 (one of fifteen children). For most of his life he was a barge captain, so it can be presumed that he learnt his trade on the canal at Gorredijk, on the barges which shipped the peat to Smilde. Rense moved to live for a time at Grootbroek and then moved on to Blokzijl.

In 1847 he managed to negotiate a lucrative major contract with the Mayor of Amsterdam to transport goods and passengers by barge on the Zuiderzee (which means Southern Sea). It was a time when the Zuiderzee was an open often hazardous stretch of water, with no dikes having been built to control the tides and water flow. (Since the Afsluitdijk was built in 1932 as a dike to separate the Zuiderzee from the open North Sea, the Zuiderzee has been known as the Ijsselmeer which means Lake Ijssel.)

Rense sailed his barge from Amsterdam to Steenwijk and back with his goods and passengers, buoyed by his municipal patronage. He was to do this for thirty years, from 1847 to 1877. He owned a house at Steenwijk, which he used as his home base, although he was more often at sea than at home. Captain van der Leij had developed a very significant reputation and was held in high esteem by all having such a prestigious and important job.

Captain Rense van der Leij

In 1832, after his first wife Grietje (Margaret) had died skating on the ice, Rense married his housekeeper, Vroutje (Veronica) Wortel (who was three months pregnant at the time of marriage). He had a further eight children with her (three at Grootbroek, three at Blokzijl and one each at Amsterdam and Steenwijk). In 1851, after she died, he then married Antje (Anna) Kolk (who was six months pregnant at the time of marriage) and they had a further six children at Steenwijk. At this time Rense was sailing to and from Amsterdam, virtually living on the barge and at intervals returning to Steenwijk to see his latest newborn (and to sow the seeds for the birth of his next child).

Gorredijk was the birthplace of Tjitse. When Rense married Veronica after Margaret's death, the family moved to Grootbroek (an area which bordered the Zuiderzee and had many canals), and then to Blokzijl. Blokzijl was a village near the open water expanses of lakes and canals at the (now known as) De Weerribber – Wieden National Park. It was the largest low-land bog of North West Europe, an area of lakes, waterways, marsh forests, reed-lands and water villages. Tjitse had the opportunity growing up in these places to spend time on the water in various vessels, sailing and paddling along the canals, through the waterways or across the lake. When he was a young man in his late teens, he was taken on occasions by his father on his barge from Amsterdam to Steenwijk, where he was not just the Captain's son, but was treated by his father as any other barge hand and had to "swab the decks" as the others did. He subsequently learnt the job of barge hand.

Tjitse's father Rense had remarried to his housekeeper Veronica when Tjitse was only eighteen months old. There was never a strong relationship between Tjitse and his stepmother. Perhaps it was that he had lost his mother when he was such a tender age, or perhaps because he had to suddenly recognize the housekeeper as his new mother. His stepmother later seemed to favour her own children ahead of her stepson and did not relate to Tjitse who was "someone else's child."

When Veronica died in 1851, Rense took Anna, (who lived in Steenwijk), as his third wife. Combined with the exposure (and love) of the ships and the sea through his father, the previously strained relationship with his stepmother, and now another stepmother that he hardly knew, Tjitse made a life-changing decision. He decided to leave home and become a sailor and sail the open, high seas of the world. He was able to sign on to a ship in Amsterdam and set sail from the Netherlands for the antipodes looking for adventure.

Shipboard life was difficult for Tjitse. On board he was no longer "the Captain's son." He was treated harshly. (It was actually no different from the way the rest of the crew were treated.) On the voyage they endured high seas (with accompanying sea sickness), oppressive heat and humidity, damp and uncomfortable conditions and were becalmed for days. Food had been of poor quality and in short supply and several of the crew were combatting various illnesses. Tjitse was beginning to question whether the decision to commit to years as a sailor had been a wise decision for him to make.

After visiting the Dutch East Indies, the ship arrived at Port Adelaide in the new colony of South Australia. Tjitse made the decision to jump ship. Whether it was planned, or a spur of the moment decision, is not known. He must have realized however that by jumping ship (which was a crime), he would probably never be able to return to the Netherlands again. Perhaps the pleasant weather with the existing blue sky, the warm rays of sunshine and the tranquil view of the distant Adelaide Hills had beckoned him. It is also known that his stepmother had died, he had no direct siblings (only stepbrothers and stepsisters), and he hardly knew his new stepmother. He rarely saw his father who was always away at sea. There wasn't a lot to return to if he eventually went back home to the Netherlands. Legend has it that Tjitse swam ashore and climbed a gum tree and did not come down until he saw the sails of his ship disappear over the horizon.

Tjitse initially made his way to Coromandel Valley in the Adelaide Hills. The Adelaide Hills area was a good hiding place in the new colony for various escaped convicts and bushrangers, many who had made their way overland from the colonies of Victoria and New South Wales in the east. One extra ship deserter in the hills would fit in easily without being too conspicuous.

The early settlers in the colony of South Australia were known as "free settlers," who had immigrated on free or heavily Government-subsidized fares. They had been promised the opportunity to buy their own land upon arrival. Many of the new settlers who had bought land had to clear the heavily wooded areas in the Adelaide Hills to be able to procure open spaces and grow crops. It was necessary for sawyers to cut down the trees, accompanied by bullock teams which cleared away the heavy wooden logs. In the Adelaide Hills the early settlers were anxious to have help to handle the bullocks as well as to have sawyers to cut down the trees. If an escaped convict or ship deserter approached them for work, no questions were asked as the free settlers needed all the help they could get. However, the settlers weren't in the position to pay much in wages, if any. Neither were the escaped convicts and ship deserters (being wanted men) in the strongest position to negotiate a better deal. Quite often the only wage given was a good supply of "tucker" to sustain the cheap labourers for another day. At an area called New Tiers (near present day Crafers), Tjitse found such work.

Tjitse was able to establish himself in the New Tiers. He had a modest accommodation which was no more than a bark shanty, where nearby he grew a few vegetables. He was managing to find work as a sawyer or as a "bullocky" (teamster). He was also learning to speak English, albeit still retaining a strong Dutch accent.

The lone Dutchman was to meet an Englishwoman, Eliza Richmond, who had immigrated with her family from England five years earlier. Her father Charles Richmond, a lace-maker from Nottinghamshire, came with his wife Eliza and eight children to South Australia on the Harpley in search of a better life. (A further two children were born in South Australia after their arrival.) Tjitse and Eliza struck up a friendship and would walk from the Adelaide Hills to the city of Adelaide to attend church services. Quite a walk!

After a time, Tjitse proposed marriage to Eliza. She was insistent that if she was to marry him, he would have to change his name from the "foreign-sounding" name to an "English sounding" name. This quite suited Tjitse, as being a ship deserter, his name would still be on the deserter's list for apprehension by the authorities. If he was to change his name, he would not only win the fair lady, but possibly no longer be searched for as a ship deserter.

He decided to call himself "John" (No more English sounding name than that!) As a surname Tjitse chose "Slater." Why Slater? In the Dutch language, the word "lei" means slate. Accordingly van der Leij loosely becomes "of the slate – or someone who works with slate, a slater."

In 1854, John Slater, aged 23, and Eliza Richmond, aged 19, married in Adelaide at Holy Trinity Church. Eliza's sister Ann and her husband Llewelyn Ford were witnesses. The newly-weds were to settle at Cox's Creek (near the present-day Bridgewater Mill) in the Adelaide Hills. John was farming, boosting his income by wood carting.

They were to have eight children together, however naming the children posed a problem. Under the Dutch tradition, the first son was named after the paternal grandfather, however their first son was named Charles after Eliza's own father on Eliza's insistence. Perhaps John Slater had felt let down, as Eliza agreed (probably reluctantly or at a weak moment), to name their second born son Rense (after John's father). So much for the traditional Dutch naming traditions. At her engagement to marry, however,

Eliza did insist on using "English sounding names." The remaining six children they had were all given "English sounding names."

In the Adelaide newspaper there was published a list of unclaimed letters, one addressed to "De Her T. van der Leij." As Tjitse was now John Slater, the letter was probably never claimed. It does however indicate that Tjitse (John) had previously made contact with his family in the Netherlands by letter to tell them that he was in South Australia. (A distant van der Leij relative Frank Jans van der Leij living in the Netherlands did recently confirm that their family at that time was always aware that Tjitse was in Australia.)

John became a lay preacher in the district. He claimed he was Baptist, however seemed to have his own version of a fire and brimstone religion. He carried his own bible with him. He had studied the bible and knew it well. He preached and gave sermons in his loud, strongly accented voice at the Ashton Memorial Church at Stirling and the Mount Lofty Bible Christian Church. When at church services, he made the children in the congregation giggle as he announced, "We shall now sing the *dirty dird* hymn."

For some reason (once again maybe due to Eliza's insistence), John decided to become naturalized. He was of Dutch birth, however now had an English sounding name, was married to an Englishwoman, was speaking English (admittedly with a Dutch accent) and living in South Australia, which was a British colony. In the colony of South Australia in the early days, Prussian Lutheran colonists had volunteered to take an oath of allegiance upon arrival at the Colony. They were not treated the same as natural born British subjects, still being technically unable to vote or buy land. They had however set a precedent for non-British subjects to commit to the Colony.

The two horses were harnessed to the big trap and John with his family were dressed up in their Sunday best clothes ready to attend the naturalization ceremony. As John started the horses and trap along the track towards Adelaide, he went a short distance, stopped for a moment, and then turned the trap around to head back in the direction from whence they had come. In answer to Eliza's immediate reaction of somewhat forceful questioning, he replied "I have changed my mind. I am going to remain a Dutchman till I die." John held prejudice against the "greedy grasping British." He had made his decision and he stubbornly wouldn't budge. The whole family including John went back to their home to change out of their Sunday best clothes.

Eliza was to die in 1872 at Crafers, bringing up blood after chasing a pig. She had been suffering from consumption (tuberculosis) for three years. Her youngest children, being two and four years old, were to be brought up by a neighbour who lived nearby. John was two years later, aged 42, to marry Mary Ann Bradley (née Hines), aged 32, who was a widow with four surviving children and worked as a midwife. They were to live in a five-roomed house with stables and unfenced garden near Crafers, on 116 acres in section 950, and were to have a further six children together. Interestingly Mary Ann allowed John to name many of the children with "Dutch sounding names." Among names used were Tjitse, Jaltia and Meatia.

John was one who enjoyed a drink. He was given the term as a "boozer" by some of the locals. (Obviously by those who didn't drink during those times, when many observed strict temperance.) It was common practice for the local market gardeners to take their produce on their horse drawn carts to the East End market in Adelaide. John would often accompany them, carrying supplies of wood to sell at the market. Much to the chagrin of their wives, many would spend most of the money earned from vegetable (or wood) sales – or even all of it – at the local public house, or any other public house on the way home. The horses would make their own way home knowing the way, pulling their inebriated driver fast asleep laying prostrate in the cart.

On one occasion on the way home from the market on the Mount Barker Road, John Slater's horses took the trolley too close to the railings of a bridge. Disaster! John lost his leg in the accident. He had unfortunately become "legless" in more ways than one! One trip to the Adelaide market too many.

Restricted by his handicap, John manufactured an artificial wooden leg to replace the one that he had lost in the accident. It is said that each year he whittled a new leg out of wood for himself, presenting it to himself as a Christmas present!

Now being physically handicapped and unable to cart wood or work as a sawyer, John made the change to become a tinsmith and made pots, pans and kettles. He travelled the Hills on a cart and horse, becoming a tinker, selling and trading his goods and doing repairs.

It was reported that John appeared in court for failing to send two of his children to school for the required 35 days for the final quarter of the year. He pleaded guilty to the charges and was fined eighty shillings, a sizeable amount which he was reluctant to pay. He did so nevertheless to avoid any further problems.

Mary Ann his wife was a stern no nonsense midwife, who had grown up in England and had been schooled by nuns. She had no time for a husband who was a drunkard and she vitriolically claimed that "he was no use to her with only one leg." She also said she had no time for a "cranky old Dutchman." (My own father, when questioned by me about the Slater family, recalled as a boy meeting John's son Rense Slater. Dad used the same term in describing him, as a "cranky old Dutchman." Dad said that he had a walking stick and if any child ventured too close, he would wildly swing at them with it. Like father, like son?)

Mary Ann was said to not be close to any of the children from John's first marriage and did not treat them well and was cruel to them. It was an unsatisfactory situation on many fronts. John and Mary Ann agreed to separate and live apart.

John lived for a while with two of his sons, Charles and Rense (both from his first marriage) in turn, and then went to live with daughter Eliza (from his first marriage). At a time when there were no government pensions for the elderly or disabled, John expected each of his sons to contribute one pound per month to support him. If they were tardy in supplying the money to him, he would reprimand them. "It's not the money only, it's the character of my boys."

Within the family there was some ill feeling. There were claims that elder daughter Ellen (Nell) did not help her father. She lived at the "Big House" at Belair with her husband Edwin Foster and seemed to be well off, yet did not assist her father financially. (She did however contribute two pounds to buy silver handles for his casket at his funeral.) Her siblings resented the fact that from a comfortable position she was not contributing, whereas they were.

Ellen (née Slater) Foster

John's wife Mary Ann continued to live apart from John. However, in a devastating bushfire the five rooms house at Crafers was destroyed, being burnt to the ground. Mary Ann had been alone at the house with her three small children. At an inquest she accused the men fighting the fire of not saving her house. In reply, those who had come to the house in order to save it had said that she told them to go away as she said there was nothing worth saving in the house other than the bed. No thanks were given to the firefighters for saving her and her children's lives, only criticism of them.

Mary Ann (née Hines) Bradley Slater

John Slater suffered heart-breaking losses within his family during his lifetime. Apart from his mother tragically dying on the ice in the Netherlands when he was young, he lost his first wife to consumption when she was a young woman. A daughter from his first marriage had died at six years of age, whereas from his second marriage, a son died at three weeks and a daughter died at three years. Tragic losses (particularly of young children) were not uncommon in those early days of the Colony.

In the Slater family also, at the age of 32 years, John's eldest son Tjitse Slater from his second marriage was later to be killed in an accident near Eagle on the Hill. It was presumed that he was kicked by one of his three horses pulling his cart and its load. It was accepted by all (and by the court at an inquest) to have been just a tragic accident. Many years later a man who was known in the district confessed on his deathbed that he had murdered Tjitse for his lead horse. The authorities never took any action.

In 1914, John Slater was eventually found dead in his bed when his daughter Eliza brought him his breakfast. He had died in his sleep. He had been confined to bed for his last three years. He was buried in his casket with silver handles in an unmarked grave at Upper Sturt Cemetery. His second wife Mary Ann was to die in 1927 of bronchitis at Bridgewater. She was buried at Stirling Cemetery (still keeping her distance from her husband).

On the inside front page of John's bible (which still exists) was written, "John Slater Vandalay [sic] born 1830 July 12 at Cor Dyke [sic] in Holland. Died September 10 1914." The misspelling of his name and birthplace was another example of the multiple spellings which occurred when translating from Dutch to English, here perhaps written in the way that John would have phonetically sounded his name and birthplace. The fact that John's date of death was also written on the front inside page in the same handwriting indicates it was not written by himself, but most probably by his second wife or one of his children.

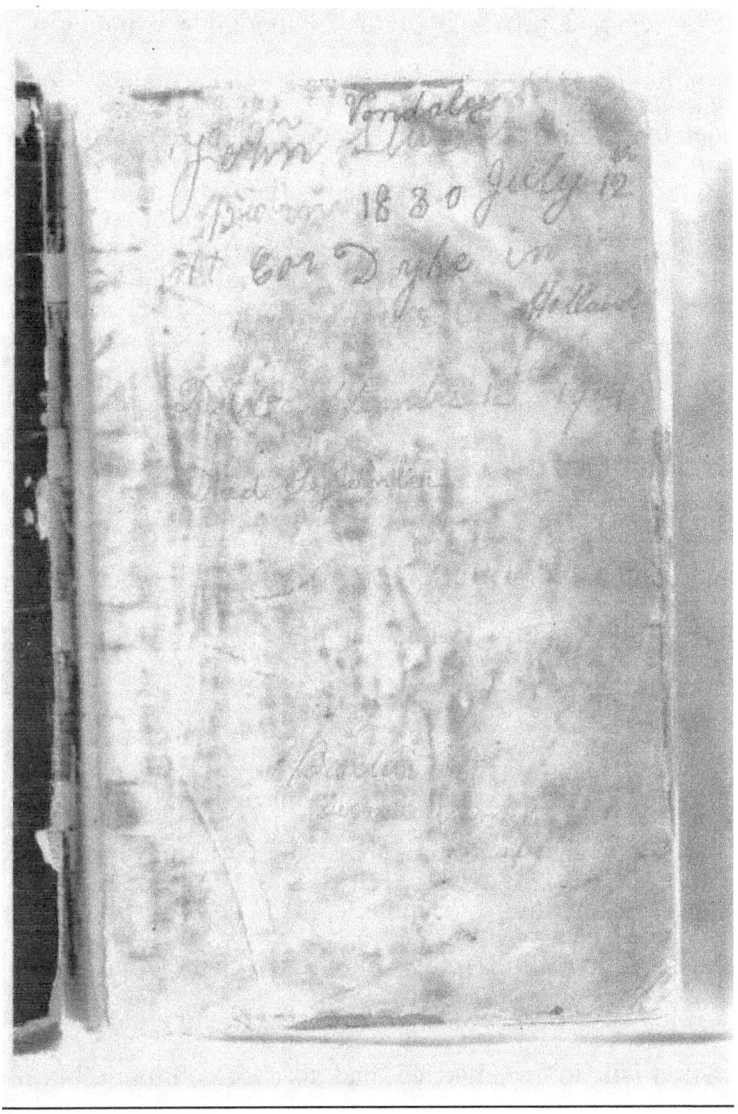

Inside page, John Slater's bible

## Conclusion:

## TJITSE RENSE van der LEIJ (1830 – 1914)
## (JOHN SLATER)

Just a name and a date? Research has shown that Tjitse was born in Friesland, a separate province of the Netherlands which was not well regarded by the other Dutch people and also had a dialect which was not easily understood. His mother tragically died when he was only six months of age and he was brought up by a stepmother who didn't care much for him. His father, who was a ship captain, was absent from home most of the time.

Why did he come to Australia? Tjitse had a difficult upbringing in several ways and probably felt he had to make his own decisions to fare for his own well-being. He became a sailor and severed all ties with his Dutch family. He became completely responsible for his own life when he decided to "jump ship" in Australia, knowing that he would probably never return to the Netherlands due to this action.

He learnt to speak English and met and married an Englishwoman, who insisted he change his name and give their children "English sounding names." Tjitse was willing to change. (This action must have taken away some of his patriotic feelings of his Dutch heritage including family naming traditions.) He became John Slater. They raised eight children together, but then his wife died. John remarried, had six more children, but then lived apart from his second wife after he lost his leg in a "boozy" accident with his cart and horse. To his credit he reinvented himself, taking up a new trade as a tinker to support his family.

Perhaps he did have a temper and was often a little "cranky." Perhaps his drinking was excessive. (He had to live with the penance of a lost limb for the rest of his life, as a result of the accident caused by his drinking.) Perhaps he was headstrong and stubborn, as displayed when he refused to undertake the naturalization ceremony.

In photographs John appeared to be a determined looking man with a ruddy complexion and a scraggy full beard. His appearance gave the impression that he perhaps may have been capable of being "cranky" on occasions.

John did have some good points. He was a "fire and brimstone" lay preacher, in his way trying to guide others to lead a better life. Tragedies had been experienced within the family, nevertheless he still carried on. He was a colourful character and was respected in the district. He was the father of fourteen children and brought them up as best he could.

In later life John was dependent on his children to care for him. He died in his sleep as a proud Dutchman, having never taken out citizenship.

He was my great great grandfather.

Thomas Bartlett

# [ 4 ]


## THOMAS BARTLETT


### 1840 – 1915

# FAMILY TREE

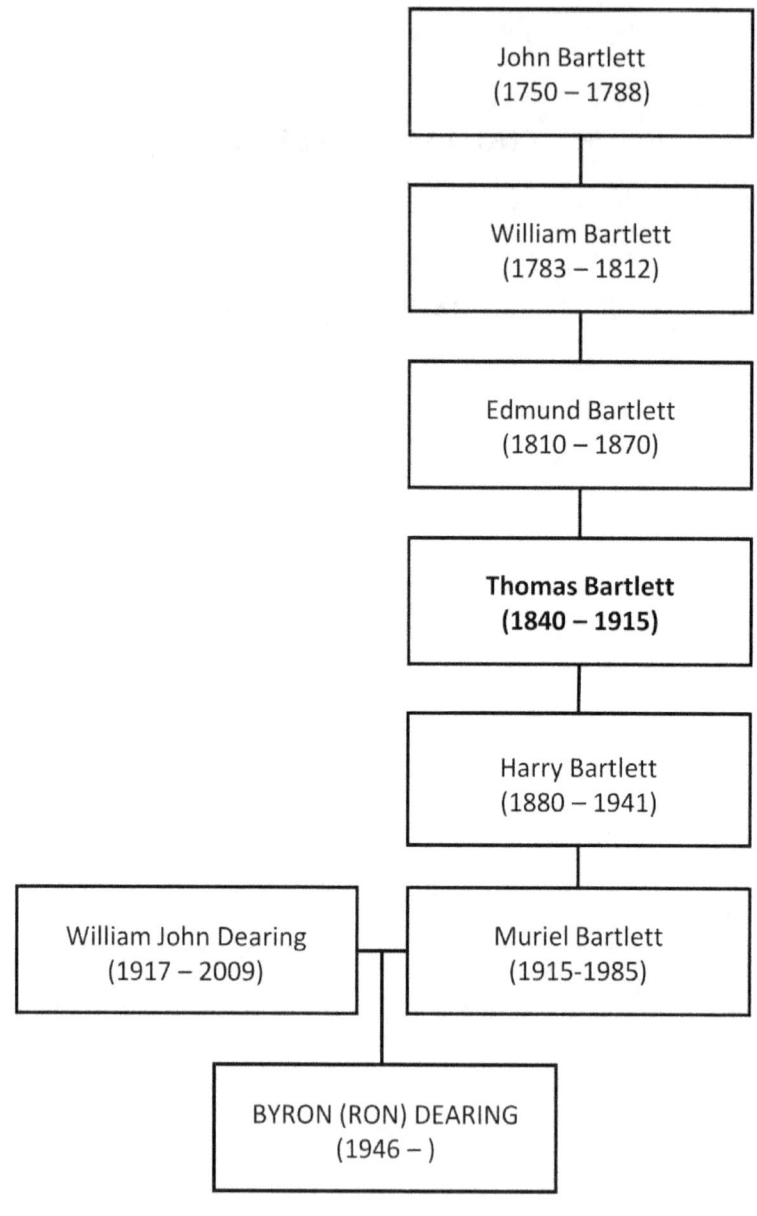

The surname Bartlett is a diminutive form of Bartholomew, of Aramaic origin meaning "ploughman, having many furrows and rich of land."

The Bartletts in my family were originally from Cornwall, England. However, they were not farmers (nor miners or fishermen), but ran a coach building business. They specialized in building carts, wagons and gipsy vans. They had a sideline in making coffins, supplying them for whenever the occasion arose.

The family lived in a small hamlet called Plushabridge, located near Linkinhorne in Cornwall where the church of the parish was situated. The church was called St. Mellor's and dated back to 981 when land was put aside for Tavistock Abbey. The present church, with its 120 feet high tower and 15th century wall paintings, was built in the 15th century. The font of the church however (in which all the Bartletts were baptized) dates to the 13th century.

13th. century church font

St. Mellor's Linkinhorne

Plushabridge was established in the late fifteenth century, having a bridge built there which crossed the River Lynher. The bridge enabled the miners from nearby Caradon mine a more convenient and shorter route to reach the church at Linkinhorne. Plushabridge is located in rural countryside, with gentle rolling hills, pleasant green pastures and bubbling streams which support the farming communities. Narrow hedge-lined roads and lanes criss-cross the countryside, leading to other hamlets and villages, few larger than Plushabridge or Linkinhorne. The River Lynher bisects the peaceful hamlet of Plushabridge, houses and cottages being either west or east of the river. In the nineteenth century copper was mined nearby, but the mines have long been abandoned.

This is the area into which Thomas Bartlett was born in 1840, to Thomas Bartlett and Elizabeth Bennett. (His actual birthplace was at nearby Starrabridge, but all the Bartletts resided at Plushabridge and Thomas spent his early days there.) Thomas was named in memory of a brother who was born in 1836 and died two years later. His father Edmund Bartlett had been born in Plushabridge at the family home of Riverside (which actually was alongside the river), where the majority of the Bartletts started their lives. Edmund's parents were first cousins, but still married despite their existing family connection. It certainly was a close-knit family!

Linkinhorne Cemetery

Riverside

The family home of Riverside however was not to stay in the ownership of the family. Uncle William Bartlett (the eldest son of the family), the owner of Riverside having inherited it, had to sell the home and farm to pay off his debts. Local farmers, perhaps after some cider(s), regularly played card games such as whist, where gambling was involved. They called it "playing for fields," where the stake in a card game would be a field that they owned. Whether William's debts were accrued due to poor farm management and business sense, unfortunate seasonal weather conditions, or by an "unlucky card hand" is not confirmed.

A marvellous letter was sent by Paul Jennings who then lived in Scotland. (Paul was a distant Bartlett relative of mine on the "English Bartletts" side.) It describes the hamlet of Plushabridge and the impressions gained by Paul through his eyes as a boy when he visited it during his school holidays. The letter brilliantly depicts the hamlet, gives an excellent insight into the way of life and captures its atmosphere. A condensed version of the letter is produced herewith:

Now my next remarks are addressed to anyone who should happen to visit Cornwall, Plushabridge in particular, as this is a kind of a guided tour.

If you approach the village (really a hamlet) from Liskeard, that is from the west, you will probably be using the lane with a very steep slope into the river valley. About a ¼ mile before you get to the bottom of the valley is a farm in which one of the Bartlett girls lived. Through the lower farm-gate you will see the former farmhouse, abandoned as a dwelling. When I was young my Uncle Will used it as a farm building to store his hay, and what an exciting place it was for me as a small boy, as we used to stay there when visiting Cornwall from Scotland. It would be interesting to find out who tenanted the place in the time of Edmund and Thomas!

At the bottom of the hill are four cottages. The one furthest south, facing onto another lane which heads back to Liskeard and joins the road we came down, is where "Jim Broad" lived with his cockatoo. I think Betsy Ann had another of these cottages, I cannot remember which. A little further into the "village" on the right is another dwelling house. If you look at it carefully, you would be correct in assuming that it used to be a chapel, the protruding bit on the left being the stable, which housed the visiting preacher's pony and trap. The baptistery, which has been removed, was fed by a local spring. The chapel was built by Francis Bartlett, who was an early member of the Christian Brethren. I remember when we used to worship there. Aunt Het used to play the tiny pedal organ, the fine booming voice of Uncle Will in the background. The chapel sadly had to close in the 1960s as people moved away or died. The present owner, though, is the proprietor of the motorcycle business just a bit further on. It's nice to reflect that there still is a local industry here, connected with transport!

Beyond this is another dwelling house, converted from the buildings associated with the Bartlett family business – workshops, store and the blacksmith shop. Note the old red letterbox in the wall with Queen Victoria's initials, "V.R." A rare sight these days. The last house on the right before the bridge, is "Riverside," where all the Bartletts were born and brought up. I have not set foot in the house since it was sold, but though there will be changes inside, the exterior has changed little.

Beyond the house down the river, used to be a great exciting wilderness known as the "Ham," which when I was a boy was a forest with massive oaks and elms, but bisected by leats and channels and old mine workings. Nothing unusual in that, you will find old copper mines all over this part of Cornwall. You will see more obvious ones up on Caradon, a hill a few miles away; the ones in the valley are more hidden in the undergrowth.

When you reach the bridge, look over the south parapet and you will see the remains of the old village well. This area used to face a lot more open, but after the house was sold, it was closed off to the public. Note also a huge circular piece of granite. This is the stone on which wheels, after being made up in the workshops, were put to be fitted with the red-hot tyres, which were made in the blacksmith shop. These tyres, having been heated in a huge open fire, close to the waiting wheel, made from brushwood from the "Ham," would be lifted, while red hot, by several men with blacksmith's tongs and dropped onto the wheel. The whole would then be immediately copiously doused with water from the river, thus achieving the dual effect of making the metal contract onto the wheel as it cooled and preventing the wood from burning. In our cottage, you will see a photograph, taken by my father in the 30s, of a miniature version of this procedure with a small wheel.

East of the bridge, the first building on the left is "our" cottage, the original bit facing the river, and an annex, built by my parents, at the back. At the bottom of the garden, nearer the river, are the remains of another blacksmith's shop, said to be where Edmund Bartlett worked. It has long been my fond wish, now having done a short blacksmithing course myself, to fully restore the building and rebuild the forge. Alas, time seems to be running out! Facing the road, just up from the cottage is the old pigsty, another project for restoration, but I don't think I shall be keeping a pig! In the old days, some livestock was kept to supplement incomes.

The field adjacent to the cottage was where the Bartletts grazed their beasts, known as "The Meadow." Each field had a name, sometimes obscure, the field on the other side of the road from the cottage was called "The Mash." Uncle Will's field opposite his house, between the two roads was more predictably known as "Tweenyways," and the one behind the chapel "Chapelfield."

Just beyond the cottage, on the same side of the road is the only house in Plushabridge built later than the 19th century, and further up, two more houses built in 1821 and 1827. Opposite these houses between granite gateposts is the narrower but more scenic route to Linkinhorne, about a mile and a half distant. *En route,* note the lovely medieval farmhouse on the left, and then another about half a mile further on. At the highest point of the road, on the left, is an ancient earthwork. Linkinhorne itself is even smaller than Plushabridge but gives its name to the parish because of the historic church. The headstones of many of the Bartlett family are found in the surrounding burial ground.

Following the death in 1936 of my great grandfather Francis Bartlett there was a general shake up and auction of most of the old furniture. My father and grandfather attended the sale, father being interested in the old family kitchen table. Joining the bidding, which was unexpectedly brisk, he got the table by raising the bid by something like five shillings to six pounds, a price so ridiculous to the mind of grandfather, a canny Scot, that he left the room in disgust, gutted by the thought that his son in law should squander such a sum on the old kitchen table. Well, I have now inherited that table, today my most prized heirloom!

A somewhat morbid reminder of the family business lies under the old kitchen table, for they used to make coffins to order. Naturally the coffin would require to be ready for the following day if at all possible, so last thing at night they would bring it into the kitchen for the final process, leaving it to dry by the kitchen fire overnight. The old kitchen tabletop was not fixed in any way, so they would just turn it face down, place the upturned coffin on it, and varnish it. Excess varnish would drip down the sides, onto the underside of the tabletop, leaving distinct patterns on the wood, so we see the outlines of many coffins on the underside of the famous table.

Before father bought the table, he was told of its history. The table was made in the workshops in Plushabridge by William Bartlett, and there were three such tables made from a single elm tree. The timber was sawn up in the saw pit there, one of these tables being presented to each of his three sons when each was married.

Questions may be asked. If this was the table presented to eldest son William, what happened to the tables presented to other sons Richard and Edmund? Do they still exist? Not much hope considering the low value put on country crafted tables in those days. Edmund obviously would not have taken his table to Australia when he immigrated.

In 1969 the family business was wound up. All the assets were sold. This marked an end to an era. The landlord sold the family home "Riverside" as well, which the Bartletts originally had built and owned, but then became tenants. My father, undaunted by his 1936 appearance, was also present at the 1969 sale (at my instigation) and I now possess many of the artefacts connected with the business, including all manner of woodworking and blacksmithing tools, of which the anvil is the crown jewel.

My mother and her sister bought a dilapidated property just the other side of the bridge from "Riverside" in Plushabridge when it came up for sale. They jointly bought it for one hundred and fifty pounds I remember and for a further twenty pounds they bought the land on which the ruined cottage next door stood. It was kept for holidays for a while, then was bought out by my parents as a place to retire to. When my parents died, I inherited the cottage and my plan was to move there on my retirement, but that plan, for one reason or another, has never materialized.

Paul offered me an invitation that if I ever travelled from Australia to England, to meet him at Plushabridge and stay at his cottage called "Pennti Myghal" (Mitchell's Cottage). His plan was to give me a mug of tea and wander with him through the garden in the early morning, past the old blacksmith forge, the pigsty, to continue down to the river, cross the bridge and explore the hamlet, see the Bartlett workshops and visit Riverside and take in the general ambience of the place.

I accepted his invitation in 2011. Accompanied by my wife, I visited him and wandered in the garden with my mug of tea. I was walking in the footsteps of my Bartlett ancestors. I saw the stains from the coffins on the underside of the kitchen table, Edmund's now ruined blacksmith shop and the pigsty, and I visited the cemetery in Linkinhorne where so many Bartletts had been laid to rest. The fact that the hamlet had changed little gave me a strange feeling as though time had stopped and I had almost been transported back to those times. It was a very special moment for me to experience, something that I look back upon fondly.

Myself with English Bartlett relatives at Plushabridge

Paul Jennings with mug of tea at Pennti Myghal

Old blacksmith shop ruins

Kitchen table with coffin varnish stains

Bartlett wheelmaking (top left – note gipsy van in background),
old wheel (top right), old pigsty (bottom)

Plushafields

In the 1841 census Thomas was shown to be living at Plushabridge with his parents, a brother, a sister as well as an apprentice blacksmith and a thirteen years old servant girl. Thomas as a growing young boy was to watch his father Edmund working at the blacksmith forge and assist where possible. The family carriage making business had the Bartlett clan filling different positions. One of Thomas' uncles was the carpenter, one was the wheelwright and of course his father was the blacksmith.

His father Edmund had been struggling to make much money for himself from his blacksmith work within the constraints of the family business. He was aware that the family coach building business would be eventually passed on by his eldest brother to his own eldest son as was the family tradition.

Edmund made the decision to move his family to Plymouth where there was apparently a lot more opportunity for work for blacksmiths in the docks and shipyards. In the 1851 census, the family were living at Stoke Damerel (near Plymouth), having a lodger to complement their income.

Thomas was keen to work to help with the family income. He had started occasional work at the age of eight years onwards. He was later able to get a job as a rivet boy on the Royal Albert Bridge which was being constructed nearby. Small boys as young as seven were used to carry the red-hot rivets up through the scaffolding to the bridge pylons for workmen to fit. (Small boys were used as they were agile and able to squeeze between the pylons and narrow gaps.) Thomas would have been older than seven, however it was dangerous work for any young boy. The red-hot rivets could inflict severe burns if they were mishandled, and an accidental fall from the bridge spans could (and did) cause severe injury or death.

The older cousin of Thomas Bartlett was also a Thomas Bartlett, who was known by an alias as "Jim Broad." He was a seaman and had travelled to Australia and spoke glowingly of Australia with its "streets paved with gold." He was an eccentric character and brought back from his voyage a yellow crested cockatoo. (There was no quarantine in those days.) What a sight he must have been, walking the Cornish countryside with an Australian cockatoo on his shoulder.

Jim Broad's encouraging comments about Australia must have influenced Edmund to immigrate with his family. Recent outbreaks locally of cholera were probably the last straw for Edmund. The decision was made. They would leave their home country, extended family and friends forever, hopefully to have a better life in the "land of opportunity."

Edmund bought the tickets for the trip to the antipodes. He paid a fee (subsidized by the South Australian Government) of two pounds for himself, his wife and his eldest son aged twenty, one pound for his daughter aged sixteen and ten shillings for Thomas aged fourteen and for his youngest son aged two. (Normal unsubsidized fare was eighteen pounds.) Edmund officially listed himself as a "labourer" not as a blacksmith, for the reason that the subsidized fare only charged two pounds for a labourer, whereas a blacksmith was charged five pounds!

Edmund Bartlett

Elizabeth Bartlett

The Lord Raglan was 923 tons, having been built in Sunderland; Captain M. Flanigan being its master. It set sail from Plymouth in July 1854. It was the 23<sup>rd</sup> ship to sail from England to the new colony of South Australia with passengers subsidized by the government. (The Lord Raglan was later to be used in transporting convicts, however it eventually caught fire and sank off the coast of Brazil.) The ship arrived at Port Adelaide in October 1854, after a 99-day voyage.

A report appeared in the newspaper the South Australian Register:

> Arrived from Plymouth on 23<sup>rd</sup> October 1854, six births and four deaths at sea and 372 souls were landed at the Colony.

Upon arrival it was necessary for the Captain to furnish a report on the voyage to the owners. The Surgeon Superintendent on board did not fare well in the report.

At a hearing investigation, Captain Flanigan reported that the Surgeon Superintendent Mr. W. Brett was deemed to be completely unable to maintain regularity or discipline and should not be recommended for any future appointments to that position. The Surgeon Superintendent had been paid a bonus for each birth that occurred on the ship; a deduction however was made from his wage for each death that occurred. Complaints were made against the Surgeon Superintendent. However, he in turn made complaints about the behaviour of a chief officer, (the first mate), regarding his conduct with one of the young female passengers.

The Immigration Board considered the matter for three days. They considered that although the officer's behaviour with the young girl had approval from both parents, officers should not have intimacies with passengers, as it set a bad example to the rest of the crew.

Thomas Bartlett's sister Elizabeth, who at sixteen was two years older than him, on the ship had met David Miller who was the ship's carpenter. She must have had some social contact with David as they were to marry two years later. If the non-contact with passengers by the crew had been more firmly enforced on the Lord Raglan, the marriage between them may not have eventuated.

Elizabeth (née Bartlett) Miller

David Miller

Edmund moved his family to Peachey Belt (now Elizabeth North), on flat farming land of 80 acres just north of Adelaide city. The area gave the opportunity for other nearby land to be bought or leased and used for farming. Thomas and his brothers helped their father on the small farm. Later as they became older, they were able to lease land themselves, Thomas leasing land at nearby Smithfield and elder brother William leasing land at nearby Penfield. A business had been set up upon arrival by Edmund that he knew well – he started a blacksmith shop. He did quite well; a blacksmith was always needed for various jobs in the new colony.

On one occasion Thomas was helping his father cutting pine trees in the Barabee Scrub. They were accompanied by a neighbour John Adair, who had brought a rifle with him. John spotted a wallaby and went to get his rifle from the dray. As he reached into the cart, the gun, which was loaded, accidentally discharged. The shot went straight through his heart. Thomas and Edmund were aghast. Nothing could be done for him. At the inquest, the finding was accidental death.

Thomas, aged 21, married Rosina Blight, aged 20, at St. George's Church at Gawler in 1861. They had their first daughter nine months after the wedding, the first of an eventual total of fourteen children.

Rosina Bartlett

Rosina was one of ten children born to Francis and Mary Blight who had emigrated from Illogan, Cornwall to South Australia on the Waterloo in 1840. Francis had been a miner back in Cornwall. Once he arrived at the colony he was classified as "destitute" and given assistance. He took the opportunity to begin farming and moved to farming land at Peachey Belt and eventually moved to Mundoora (near Redhill) to farm. Once again it was proved in the new colony that if one was willing to work, one could survive.

Rosina, a twin, had been born in 1841 in Currie Street in Adelaide. It is suggested that she was part of the first set of white twins born in the Colony. It was reported that the aborigines living at Pinky Flat on the River Torrens came to Currie Street to see the newly born twins. It was such a curious event for them, and after a close examination they said to the mother "You very good white lubra – two picaninnies".

In 1863, Thomas moved from the farm to start his own blacksmith business at Glenelg, the seaside village where in 1836 the colony of South Australia had been proclaimed. David Miller (the ship's carpenter who had married Elizabeth, the sister of Thomas) had established a thriving timber and iron business at Glenelg. David was instrumental in building the Glenelg Town Hall, and eventually had a street corner and (then) railway stop on Jetty Road named after him. It was known as Miller's Corner (on the corner of Jetty Road and Partridge Street).

Miller's Corner

Thomas was to sell the blacksmith business at Glenelg after about three years. He did not wish to spend the rest of his days working over a dirty anvil and hot coals. To own and farm the land was his dream and passion. He went back to farm on leased land at Grace Plains with his elder brother William and younger brother Edmund.

In the South Australian Register newspaper in August 1870 the following advertisement appeared:

> FOR SALE, at PEACHEY BELT, near Penfield, an Acre of Land, on which is erected Two Good DWELLING-HOUSES – one of Five Rooms, with Cellar, and one of Four Rooms, with Cellar; also BLACKSMITH'S SHOP of Three Forges, with Good WHEELWRIGHT'S SHOP, and other necessary buildings. The above being in one of the best districts offers a good opportunity to

a person wishing to establish himself in a good Business. A good part of the purchase-money can remain at 8 percent. Stock and Tools can be taken on terms that may be agreed upon. The Business has been established for 16 years, and the present proprietor is obliged to give up through ill-health. Title can be seen and all particulars obtained by applying to Mr. Edmund Bartlett, blacksmith, near Penfield.

The business was bought by engineer and undertaker Joseph Blake. (The current suburbs Blakeview and Blake's Crossing are named after him.)

Edmund was to die at his residence two months after submitting the advertisement in 1870. (He was probably one of undertaker Joseph Blake's first customers at Peachey Belt.) His death certificate stated congestion of the liver and constipation of the bowels as the cause of death. He was buried at the nearby Zoar Pioneers Cemetery, alongside the Zoar Methodist Church (which was demolished in 1958). Two years later his widowed wife Elizabeth was to marry a widower Thomas Sluman Lyle, who was originally from Cornwall.

The Strangways Act of 1869 passed by parliament enabled crown lands to be sold on a twenty percent deposit and balance paid before four years. Maximum ownership was 640 acres. Thomas Bartlett initially bought 313 acres in the Dublin hundred section of Gawler in 1871 and settled at Grace Plains. His elder brother William bought 640 acres in 1873 whereas brother-in-law David Miller (husband of Elizabeth Bartlett) bought 640 acres in 1871 and 1873, both also in the Dublin Hundred.

They farmed the lands, however the Strangways Act was repealed and replaced by the Crown Lands Consolidation Act, which allowed ownership of more acreage. The Bartletts and David Miller sold their lands at the Dublin hundred. Thomas and David Miller bought land to farm at Stockyard Creek in the Mid North in 1875, whereas William bought land to farm at Telowie in 1877. Younger brother Edmund was also later to buy land at Owen near Stockyard Creek.

Thomas was to farm at Stockyard Creek for 22 years. At Stockyard Creek, he was to own up to 1361 acres (whereas David Miller owned up to 1119 acres). Part of the land was agricultural; the remainder was for first-class grazing. It was mostly fenced but the fencing was somewhat out of repair at the time the property was purchased. Eventually all of Thomas' land was enclosed; 500 acres was in crop, and he had good stone cottages and a reservoir. (Both Thomas and David were to lose some land for the railway to be run through their properties in 1880.) A new nearby railway siding for loading grain onto the railway trucks to convey the wheat by train to Hamley Bridge was installed, which proved to be a godsend. In 1881 both Thomas and David had fully paid off their lands and they were freehold.

Stockyard Creek had become the established family farm for Thomas and Rosina. Further to the two children born at Peachey Belt, the two born at Glenelg and the four born at Grace Plains, they were to have a further six children at Stockyard Creek. A son had sadly died at aged seven and another son had died at three months. Tragic occurrences such as these which were huge setbacks for Thomas and Rosina, but having other children in their family to care for and a farm to run, life had to continue on.

121

The Council held a meeting at nearby Owen regarding opening a public road through the Thomas Bartlett property to the Stockyard Creek Railway Station. Thomas asked for seven and a half pounds per acre for the land, but the Council were only able to pay six pounds per acre. Council would have to also pay for fencing for the length of 180 chains. Thomas agreed to accept the offer of six pounds per acre "for the good of the people." His cooperation with the Council and showing to be a good and honest farmer was to pay dividends in later years. He was selected as a councillor and later as a chairman at the Dalkey Council, being thought of by the other councillors as capable, responsible and was well respected.

A survey was conducted by Arthur Henry Smith regarding sections 92 and 219 hundred of Dalkey (near the actual creek and the Stockyard Creek Railway Station). The intention was to establish a township to be named "Bartleville" after the owner of the land, Thomas Bartlett. Among the streets proposed were Rosina Street (named after his wife), Mary and Emma Streets (named after his two eldest daughters) and Lyle Street (named after his mother who had remarried a Lyle). The completed survey remained waiting for action to be taken for future development.

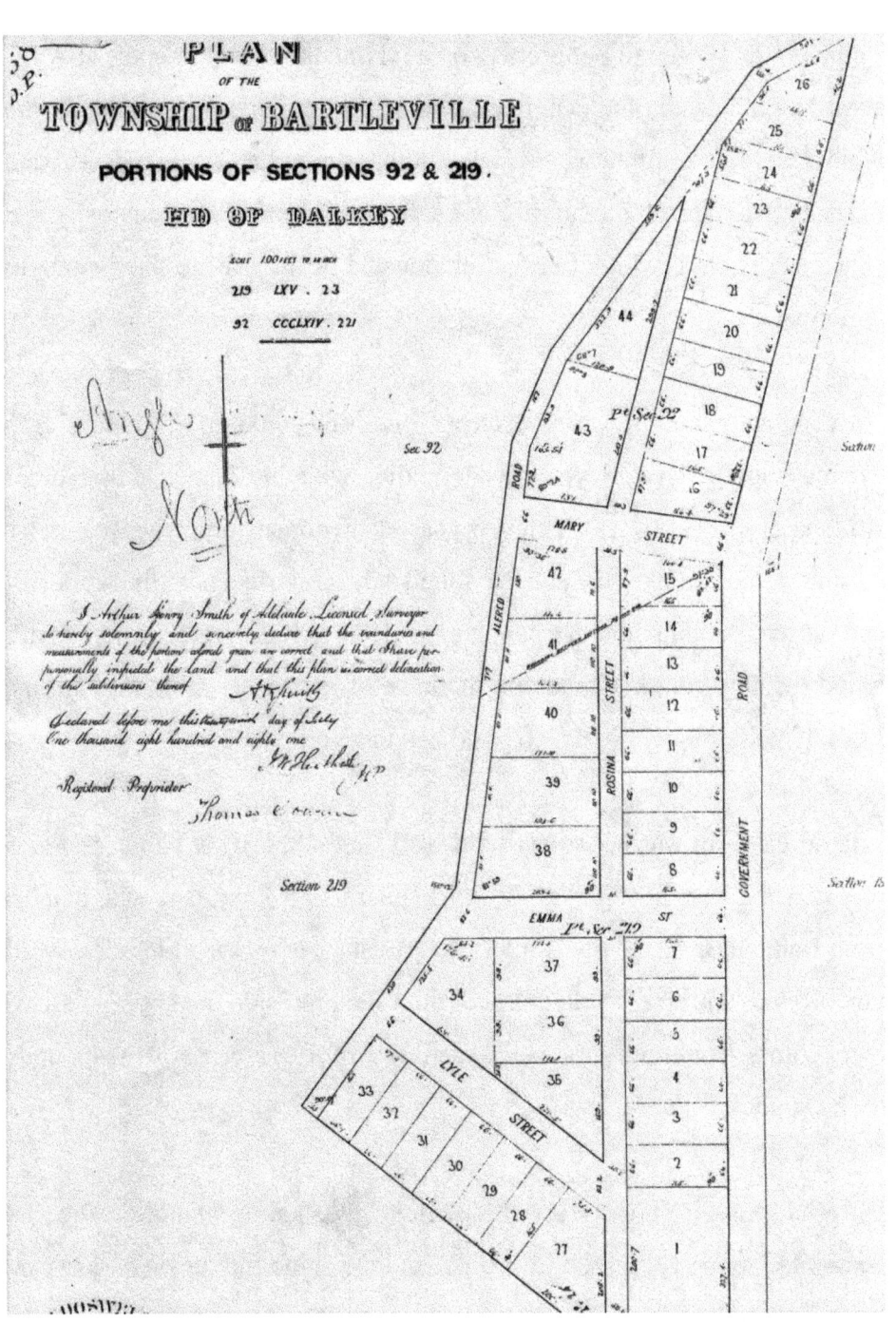

Survey of Bartleville

123

Thomas was chosen to be foreman on a jury at an inquest in court at Alma regarding the death of a local man. It was an extremely sad situation as the widow was left destitute with small children to care for. The jury found that the death was a result of natural causes. In an example of his generosity and character, Thomas without hesitation donated his jury fee to the distraught widow.

Growing up on a farm was an exciting life for the children of Thomas. Son Thomas junior aged eleven loved mixing with his Dad and the other workers on the farm. As an eleven-year-old, Thomas junior was naturally curious, as boys are of that age. He found a dynamite cap near the workmen and started prodding it with a pen. It exploded. He was severely injured with blood rushing from his hand and the bone of his hand visible through his flesh. His first finger on his left hand had to be amputated.

Life on the farm was not solely hard work and no play for Thomas. It was reported that he challenged a Mr. P. Hoepner to a trotting race with horses, from Hamley Bridge to the Alma Hotel, a distance of three miles. The word got around and the locals turned out, lodging side bets on the two competitors. The most anticipated race was to offer a prize of two pounds to the winner.

Unfortunately for Thomas (and his previously cashed-up supporters) he was beaten by about 100 yards in a time of about nine minutes. (At least he wasn't "gambling for fields" like his Uncle William had tended to do back in Plushabridge in Cornwall!)

Thomas was a member of the local shooting club at Hamley Bridge. There were some rabbits on his property and Thomas and his sons refined their shooting skills by keeping the rabbit population down, as well as shooting the occasional trespassing fox or wild pig.

Working on a farm was hard, backbreaking work, often in extreme heat or bitter cold. There was an unsubstantiated rumour that Thomas kept a flagon of wine hidden away in the hut in the far end paddock. After ploughing the paddocks, he would often finish near the far end paddock and have a quiet tipple. The rumour was "kept under wraps" by his family, who did not want Thomas, who was a pillar at the local church (known for its strict temperance attitude), to be known as "an imbiber of the evil drink."

The elder brother of Thomas was William. He was to ultimately fall to much lower depths than Thomas due to the "evil drink." He had been farming at Telowie (north of Stockyard Creek) for many years. On a visit to the coastal port of Port Pirie, William mysteriously went missing and could not be found after several thorough searches by locals. Witnesses said that he was last seen drinking rather freely at the local Royal Exchange Hotel with friends and had been in good spirits. Seventeen days later his body was found by a fisherman, floating in the river near the BHP wharf.

At the Knapmans Hotel, an inquest held by Mr. F. C. Crocker JP returned a verdict of "found drowned." It was revealed that in a story printed by a local newspaper, his life had recently been insured for 1100 pounds, a portion of which was only taken out a few weeks earlier.

It was a struggle for Thomas to keep his farm going after several years of severe droughts. It was a frustrating time for all farmers. In 1865, a surveyor George Goyder had drawn up on a map a somewhat crooked line roughly going from west to east across South Australia. The crooked line became known as Goyder's Line. Goyder had studied the records of annual rainfall averages in the colony. His warning was that above (north) of the line, crops should not be grown as those areas averaged less than ten inches of rain annually. Below (south) of the line the land was arable for crops.

After some good rainfall seasons, some farmers ignored the advice and started growing crops north of the Goyder Line. They believed the theory that "rain follows the plough." When the severe droughts struck, many farmers above (north of) the Goyder line had to abandon their farms and walk off the land. It was only a line drawn on a map, but it was to markedly effect the livelihood of so many farmers and their families. Fortunately for Thomas, he was farming below (south of) the Goyder Line. However, farming for him was still a struggle.

Thomas was trying to promote the surveyed Bartleville as a likely location for a new town, even offering to donate land to the Council for the building of council chambers there. He made an offer to fence the land and transport the necessary stone for building the chambers to the site. The Council did not accept the offer.

An application was made by a Mr. Thomas Cowan to the Licensing Board to run a public house at the Stockyard Creek railway station, to be called the Railway Hotel. However, it was rejected, being judged not required as there would be no accommodation available. The government also did not wish to spend taxpayers' money on the railway station as there was another established railway station at nearby Owen.

A meeting of creditors with Thomas was called at the office of H.E. and H.J. Downes in Waymouth Street, Adelaide. The balance sheet produced showed liabilities of 5571 pounds. Assets were shown as 6017 pounds, a surplus of only 446 pounds. Thomas had struggled financially through several barren seasons and he (and they) could see the "writing on the wall." The establishment of the township of Bartleville was more than likely not to go ahead and appeared doomed, nearby Owen probably to be preferred. Thomas realized he had to sell the Bartleville land.

In the Adelaide Register newspaper in September 1879 the following advertisement was lodged:

THE TOWNSHIP OF BARTLEVILLE.

B. DORNWELL, under instructions from Mr. Thomas Bartlett, will sell – All that piece of LAND, being portion of Sections Nos. 219 and 92, HUNDRED of DALKEY, comprising 44 ALLOTMENTS, laid out in the quarter, half, and one acre blocks as the TOWNSHIP OF BARTLEVILLE, situated and adjoining the Railway Station and Goods Shed between Hamley Bridge and Balaklava (the only stations between those places). The township should commend itself to Wheatbuyers, Millers, Storekeepers, Speculators, and others, as it is the centre of a large and fertile Agricultural District, and is on the junction of nine main roads, and adjoining the only Railway

Station on the line for over twenty-two miles. There is on the land adjoining in the Creek an unlimited supply of superior BUILDING STONE AND SAND.

There is also a plentiful supply of FRESH WATER adjoining the Township from a WELL and GOVERNMENT RESEVOIR, the latter capable of holding 2,000,000 gallons, as well as an unlimited supply of timber.

Terms 20% cash balance 2 years being interest 7% p.a.

Plan and further particulars at Auction Centre, also Weatherboard Home (iron roofing) of three rooms and detached kitchen adjoining the above land and quite new last year. Also 800 fat wethers, 10 draught horses – terms for stock horses at sale.

N.B. The first train from Adelaide in the morning of the sale will convey intending purchasers from Hamley Bridge to Bartleville.

After the advertisement had appeared several times in the newspaper, it was eventually reported in the local newspaper by the auctioneer Mr. B. Dornwell that the 44 allotments were sold at the surveyed township of Bartleville at the Stockyards Passenger and Goods Station between Hamley Bridge and Balaklava at extremely good prices, bringing from 13 pounds to 300 pounds per acre. He also reported there were sold 800 sheep at 1 shilling and 9 pence, ten horses ranging from 8 pounds to 38 pounds. Attendance was good and the bidding was brisk.

The proposed township of Bartleville had been sold, yet at a "farming land" price, not a "new town subdivision price," despite the positive slant given in the newspaper sales report from the auctioneer (forever a salesman).

The establishing of the township of Bartleville never did go ahead. The nearby town of Owen was chosen to be developed as it had a grander expansion plan including a town square grid and surrounding parkland area. Had the plan for Bartleville been more likely to eventuate, Thomas would have sold his farmland at an obviously greater financial advantage.

(The current owner of Bartleville at Stockyard Creek lives in the Bartleville farmhouse. His father had put a framed copy of the Bartleville survey on the wall in his lounge room. Interestingly, the owner and his father initially did not know who Thomas Bartlett was when approached. They knew the Bartleville survey story of the property they now owned, but not the man behind it.)

Thomas kept farming in the Stockyard Creek area, yet continually struggled with drought affecting his crops. He was subsequently also struggling financially. By order of the mortgagee, his remaining farmland was advertised for sale in 1887. In 1889, Thomas himself put what remaining land he had up for sale. Thomas continued on, having to contend with a major mice plague in 1890, continual droughts and poor seasons, as well as the occasional bushfire. He wanted to move to near Hamley Bridge. The land there was more suitable for stock, rather than crops, which were so affected by drought. Thomas was planning to raise lambs to be sold to the Adelaide market.

In January 1897, the following advertisement appeared in the Adelaide Register newspaper:

AUCTION

On Monday 26<sup>th</sup> January at 1 o'clock sharp.

ON THE FARM KNOWN AS MR. THOMAS BARTLETT'S, STOCKYARD CREEK

DAVID VIRGO is instructed to sell by auction without reserve, in consequence of his having let the farm.

The whole of his LIVE and DEAD stock now on the farm consisting of

11 head good farm horses, 6 head cattle including some really good cows, about 30 sheep, 3 reaping machines, 1 winnower, 1 wagon (old), 2 three furrow ploughs, 2 plain land ploughs, 3 double furrow ploughs, 1 single plough, 3 land rollers, 1 scarifier, 2 sets of harrows, 1 seedsower and chaffcutter, buggy (old), spring-dray (old), 1 set swings, 14 assorted harnesses, about 25 tons of Wheaton hay, about 10 tons Stack Oaten hay, about 1000 bags wheat chaff, heaps of heads, 2 bags screenings, 10 bags seed wheat, 10 bags purple straw, 80 bags Darts Imperial straw, about 30 tons Algerian oats, about 30 tons firewood, lot fencing posts, and host of useful sundries.

For – absolute clearance, terms cash, no reserve. No other stock admitted.

Refreshments provided.

The land and stock of the Thomas Bartlett property was eventually sold. The opportunity arose for Thomas to buy a property at Corcondo (near Hamley Bridge) which had a sizeable house, "Corcondo House," on the property. Thomas could buy the property, perhaps lease extra land if the sheep farming was successful and could buy extra parcels of land when they became available.

Thomas bought the property in 1897. The family moved from Stockyard Creek to Corcondo. With two grown up sons about the place and three keen teenagers willing to help, the farm thrived. Thomas issued a warning in the local newspaper that any horses or cattle that strayed onto his property would be sent to the local pound. Pigs that strayed onto his property would not fare as well – they would be shot! He did indeed produce fine lambs for the Adelaide market and with his expertise backed by experience in agriculture saw him develop a reputation as one of the district's foremost crop producers.

In 1902 it was reported in the local newspaper that there had been a fire at the Bartlett Corcondo farm. At breakfast, a spark from the fire fell on the thatched roof of the underground dairy and set fire to it. Most of the stored produce was lost.

The Bartlett sons started playing cricket for Hamley Bridge, but soon realized that there were enough players locally to field a team at Corcondo. The Corcondo Cricket Club was formed with Thomas Bartlett as president and his son Thomas (junior) Bartlett as captain. With the four youngest sons of Thomas regularly putting in top match-winning performances, the

Corcondo team proved quite formidable in the district, dominating and winning almost all of its matches. This was despite the Corcondo area not having the population of the towns and subsequently the extra players to choose from. An example of their dominance was reported in the local Kapunda Herald newspaper:

> 17 February – Alma all out 223. Corcondo. with only one hour and twenty minutes to bat before stumps, no wicket for 242. (F. Bartlett 129 n.o. H. Bartlett 108 n.o.)

When there wasn't a cricket match scheduled, the Bartlett sons played tennis enjoying similar success, joining some of their sisters on the courts as the competition was a mixed one. If it was harvest time, the farmers were far too busy to be playing sport on Saturdays, so the matches were cancelled. No sport was played on Sundays, as Sundays were for going to church.

In 1906 it was reported that Thomas Bartlett lost 300 acres of stubble in a bushfire which may have started from cinders or sparks from a passing train. Thomas had fortunately just reaped his crop and it was not lost or damaged.

At aged 69, Thomas decided it was time for retirement. With the assistance of his sons, he had built his farm at Corcondo to 1081 acres; 685 acres owned and 396 acres leased. He had enjoyed some drought-free years with his crops and his sheep and raising of lambs had been particularly successful. His plan was to sell Corcondo and move to the city of Adelaide for his retirement.

In the Adelaide Register newspaper in March 1909 the following advertisement was lodged:

## CLOSING SALE

on farm Corcondo 2 miles from Hamley Bridge on the Alma Road. Bagot Shakes & Lewis Ltd. have received instructions from Thomas Bartlett whose farm they have sold to sell without reserve The Whole of stock.

23 horses include 5 draught mares (in foal to good stallions), 10 gelded and dry mares, 4 good yearlings, 2 foals, 1 roadster, 1 trap mare.

6 cattle include 4 good milk cows, 2 heifers.

220 fat wethers (in lots to suit purchasers).

Implements. 2 harvesters, 2 strippers, 25 furrow ploughs, 2 drills, trolley and hay frame, 2 trip drays, 2 ploughs, winnower and elevator, 2 chaff cutters, 2 land rollers, 2 sets wheatscreens, 2 traps (1 hooded), blacksmith tools, anvil, bellows, tongs, etc. 3 cwt. barbed wire, 7 tanks, quantity red gum posts, and strainers, handtruck, bag lifter.

65 tons of good hay

Plough harness, trap harness.

The whole of up-to-date furniture, together with a host of Sundries to be found on a well-equipped farm, too numerous to mention

Luncheon provided.

Terms – as usual and special terms for Harvesting Material at sale.

Old farm machinery at Corcondo

Thomas was definitely retiring from farming, selling his farm and all of his stock, farm implements and "sundries too numerous to mention." Corcondo and contents were duly sold and the Thomas Bartlett family moved to "the big smoke" (Adelaide). Enough money had been received through the sale of the Corcondo farm that Thomas was able to buy four relatively modern houses in the city. Three were in Croydon, one in Woodville, all west of the city towards the coast. As his three younger boys (Harry, George and Frederick) had worked extremely hard for many years at Corcondo for no wages, just board and meals, Thomas and Rosina decided to give them each a house in Adelaide to live in. The question was raised: Who gets which house?

It was to be decided by a coin toss. The coin toss for the houses was made. Harry called heads and won the house at Woodville which had a tennis court. (Thomas and Rosina had already chosen one of the houses in Croydon.) There was however much consternation. One of the other brothers (and particularly his wife) had set their hearts on the tennis court house. Harry could see that there would always be continual friction, bickering and bad feelings among the family, so he gallantly offered the Woodville tennis court house to his disgruntled brother and took his pick of the two remaining Croydon houses.

The money that Thomas had made in selling Corcondo not only bought four houses, but some of the money that was left over was put by Thomas in to buying some vacant land in the district. This land was donated to the Churches of Christ at Hindmarsh. They had been wanting to build another church somewhere in the developing Croydon district.

The foundation stone for the Croydon Church of Christ in Elizabeth Street was laid by Thomas at a well-attended ceremony. He was presented with a silver trowel. The church was to have a stone base with superstructure of wood and two classrooms as well as a baptistry under the platform. Cost to be 844 pounds, with Brown Bros. the contractor, Mr. T. Tatum the architect and the Reverend Horsell to be the first minister. (The Croydon Church of Christ was to last for over one hundred years. It was the church where my parents were married and where my mother's funeral was held. It was eventually demolished to make way for the new North-South expressway at Croydon.)

Croydon Church of Christ

Foundation stone laid 1911

Congregation Croydon Church of Christ

138

Thomas and Rosina celebrated their golden wedding anniversary (fifty years) in 1911. An excellent photo was taken of them and their ten surviving children as a group and was published in the "Chronicle" newspaper. (See photo left, with them at front centre.)

Thomas Bartlett was to die in 1915. He was buried in the Cheltenham Cemetery (near Port Adelaide). Probate was granted in 1916 for an amount of 4,400 pounds. He was later to be joined in the grave by his wife Rosina, who died in 1929. At the time of Rosina's death, she had 46 grandchildren and 44 great grandchildren.

The gravesite lease was not renewed by the family and the grave was reused. The tombstone was transferred to the Bartleville property at Stockyard Creek in 2015 (one hundred years after Thomas' death), by local farmer Ray Marshman the present owner of Bartleville. (His house also had the framed survey of Bartleville on the wall in the lounge room.) It was interesting to note that from a very large family, it was a "non-relative" who took custody of the tombstone.

Thomas Bartlett grave

Thomas Bartlett tombstone

Conclusion:

## THOMAS BARTLETT (1840 – 1915)

Just a name and a date? Research has shown that Thomas was born into a close-knit family in a pleasant rural countryside in Cornwall, England. (The family was so close-knit that his grandparents had married being first cousins!) He started working at eight years of age and was then taught by his father the blacksmith trade. Thomas had an excellent upbringing, being taught family benevolence and responsibility.

Why did he come to Australia? His father Edmund could not see much future in England as the family carriage building business was not to be passed on to him. There appeared more opportunities for a blacksmith in the colonies. At fourteen years of age, Thomas experienced the adventure of a voyage to Australia when the family decided to immigrate. He thrived on this opportunity to go to Australia, where he plied his blacksmith trade and then farmed.

He married (a marriage which lasted over fifty years) and had fourteen children in what was a close family. (The fact that his sons worked on the farm for no wage showed that they were working for the family's benefit and not wanting to be leaving home for their own benefit. Thomas saw that they were eventually well rewarded once the farm was sold.) On the farm he fought drought, mice plagues and bushfires. At one stage he was almost bankrupt. He experienced some tragedies. Yet, with the support of his wife Rosina, had the determined spirit to continue on. With his sons helping on the farm, he became a successful farmer in the Hamley Bridge district and Council chairman and councillor in the Dalkey district, as well as president of the Corcondo Cricket Club.

Upon retirement Thomas moved to Adelaide, buying four houses and giving one to each of his three sons. He also bought land and contributed to the building of the Croydon Church of Christ on that land which he donated. (It can be considered that if Thomas had not sold the farm and moved to Croydon where he established the Croydon Church of Christ, I may not even exist! My mother met my father at the Croydon Church of Christ.) Thomas died in 1915 and was buried at Cheltenham Cemetery.

In photographs Thomas appeared to be a man with stocky build and a long white "Ned Kelly" beard. In his late years he used a walking stick. He was an early pioneer, hard-working respected farmer, chairman of the Council, a generous patron and founder of the local church, as well as a loving husband and a perfect role model as father to his children.

He was my great grandfather.

Arthur Giscard Jarvis

# 5

# ARTHUR GISCARD JARVIS

## 1862 – 1940

# FAMILY TREE

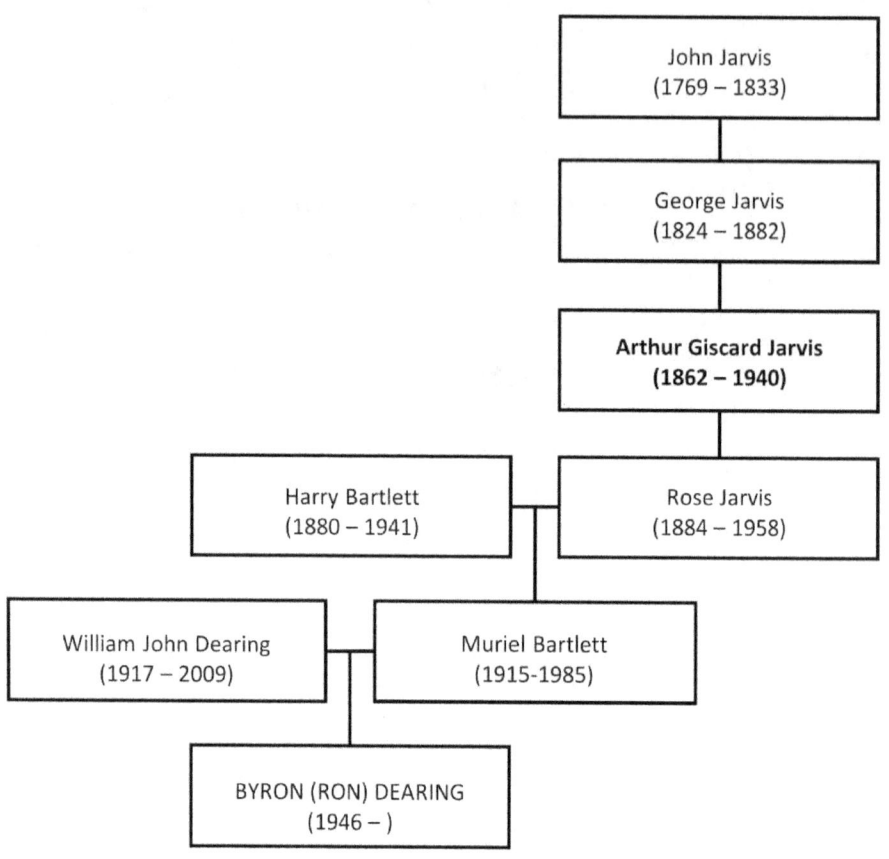

The name Jarvis had many types of spelling, but it is generally agreed that that it came from the forename "Gervais" meaning "man with a spear."

The Jarvis family have been traced back to Wisbech in Cambridgeshire, England, where Arthur's grandfather John, who was a cooper, lived in North Brink, Wisbech. Wisbech was known as "the capital of the Fens." It was an old market town and inland port, being on the tidal River Nene. It was reported in the year 664 that land at Wisbech was granted to the Medeshamstede (now Peterborough) Abbey. The word "Wisbech" means "bank by the marshy meadow."

The maternal grandmother of Arthur Giscard Jarvis was Frances (Fanny) Giscard, from a French Huguenot family which had fled France to come to England in the late 1600s. King Louis XIV had revoked the 1598 edict of Nantes in Fontainebleau in 1685, which meant French Protestants would have to convert to Catholicism or flee the country as refugees. Many Huguenots fled France across the English Channel to England because of the religious persecution.

The Giscard family were renowned clockmakers. The trade and wealth of experience was passed through generations of Giscards. When they came to England they brought with them their clockmaking skills. Many Giscard clocks (and watches) still exist in various parts of England. A Giscard clock or watch is now a very valuable and sought-after antique, worth quite a lot of money.

A Giscard clock and watch

Arthur Giscard Jarvis was the youngest of nine children, born to George Jarvis and Elizabeth Headin in 1862. His father was a baker in Wisbech and, as a young man, Arthur helped in the bakery and learnt the trade. The 1871 census shows that Arthur was a scholar living with his parents and three brothers at Wisbech. In the 1881 census the family had moved to York, Yorkshire, George listed as a baker and Arthur listed as a confectioner. George was to die in 1882 of cancer of the tongue. Arthur continued to work in the bakery/confectionery shop attached to their dwelling.

Arthur had met Mary Moore who was the daughter of Yorkshireman Joe Moore, a labourer/textile worker and previous ginger beer maker. In the 1881 census Mary was listed as a servant to Baptist minister Ron Cook and his young family at Micklegate, York. Two years later the same minister was to marry Mary, aged 22, and Arthur, aged 21, at the Baptist Chapel at York. Arthur and Mary had a child (a daughter), in York.

They then moved to London in the late 1880s where two more children were born. Family folklore suggested that Arthur worked in the bakery at Buckingham Palace, but it is more likely that he worked at one of the many bakeries in London near where they were living at Dulwich. It is difficult to imagine Queen Victoria sampling the cream cakes made by Arthur (by Royal Appointment, exclusively for her!).

The family returned to York and after a time Arthur sold his shop and dwelling at Cherry Street. Arthur had found a new shop to continue his work in the bakery/confection trade. He had managed to acquire a shop in Micklegate in an excellent and very busy location. Micklegate was an ancient, historic street which ran from the city wall to the River Ouse in the centre of York. The exit at Micklegate Arch through the city wall to outside the city of York was quite near the shop. The bakery also sold confectionery, groceries and drinks and did deliveries.

There exists a magnificent photo taken in the early 1890s of Arthur with his family in front of the shop at Micklegate. It shows Arthur with wife Mary nursing her child, Mary's sister Rose Hannah, an unknown gentleman (who could be one of Arthur's brothers), Arthur's son Ernest and his daughter Rose (my grandmother), as well as the delivery boy. (It is one of my all-time favourite photos, supplied to me by Brian Collard, distant English Moore relative.)

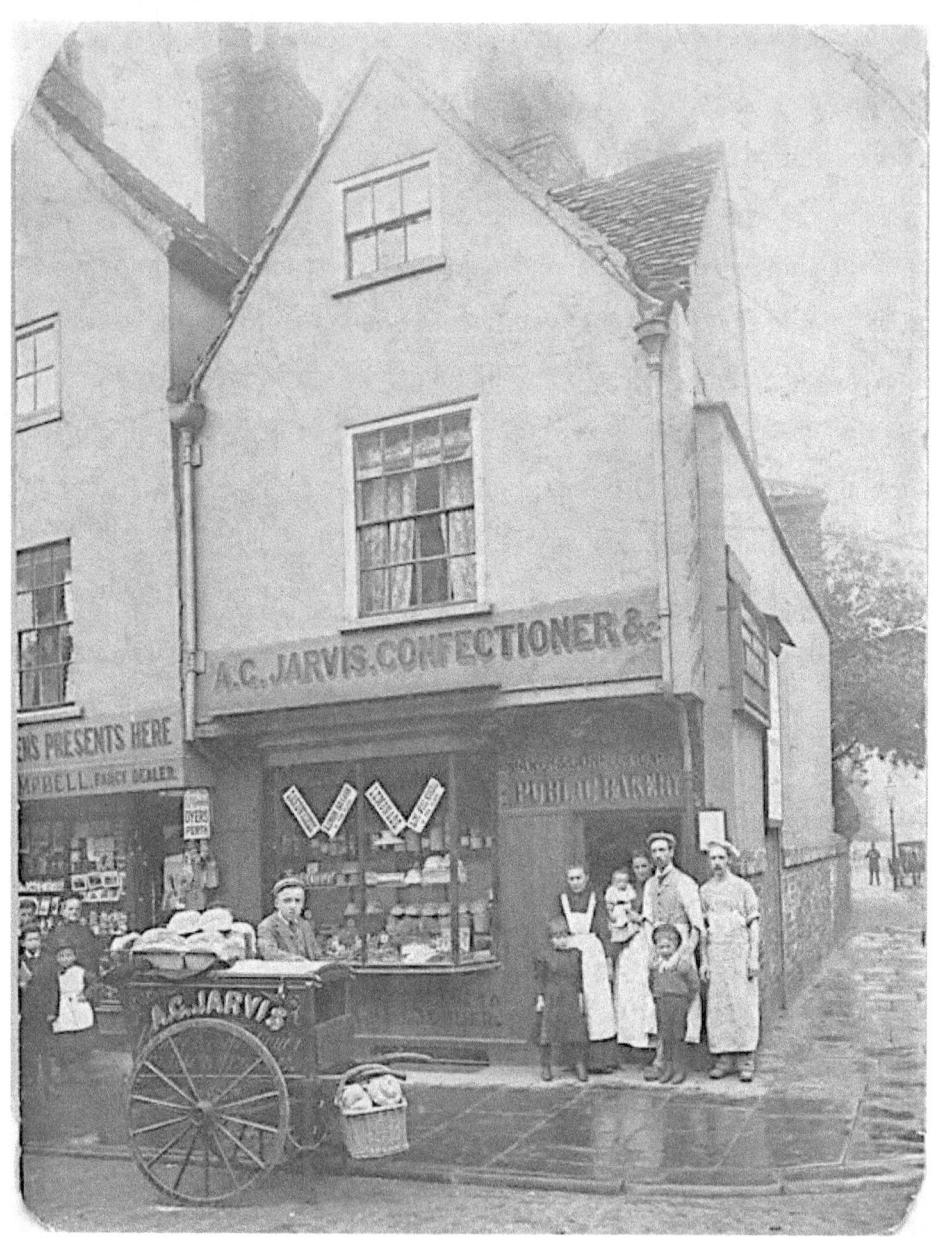

The Jarvis shop at Micklegate

When I visited York with my wife in 2011, we made our way to the address of 31 Micklegate. Google Earth had shown the old baker shop to be a party hire shop. However, we were surprised when we arrived at the site to discover that it was now a barber shop. The barber shop had only opened three weeks before and the barber was surprised that we Australians knew more about the shop than he did! He was pleased to show us around. The shop appeared to have few minor structural changes from what was depicted in the photo when Arthur and his family worked there. I had my photo taken standing on the same front doorstep on which Arthur and his family had stood to have their photographs taken over one hundred years prior.

Brian Collard, the barber and myself at the shop

My wife Robyn at the Micklegate shop

Three children were born in York. However, in 1895 their son Richard Henry, who had been born four years prior, died and was buried at York Cemetery. Arthur's wife Mary was depressed after the loss of her son. She was also struggling with illness in the cold wet climate of Yorkshire and she particularly dreaded the winters. She suffered from asthma, and attacks were becoming more severe and more frequent.

At this time Arthur's brother John William Jarvis had already immigrated to Australia. From his letters he wrote positive reports of the potential of Australia and its wonderful climate. Arthur, concerned about his wife's health, made the decision to immigrate to Australia. It would hopefully be a better climate for his ailing wife in the warmer conditions. He had a trade as a baker and he felt sure there would be opportunities for work in that field. Also being in Australia he considered would be good for their children's upbringing. His decision to immigrate to Australia was made despite his bakery business at Micklegate doing extremely well at the time.

The Jarvis family set sail from London via Capetown to Melbourne in 1898 on the S.S. Aberdeen, mastered by Captain A. Robb. Arthur had given his occupation as a builder, not a baker. Whether that increased his chances for acceptance for immigration, or whether builders were charged a lesser fare for the voyage is not known. (The S.S. Aberdeen was built by the British, later sold to the Ottoman Empire and in World War I was ironically sunk by a British submarine.) Upon arrival at Melbourne the family then took the steamer Marloo to Adelaide, arriving in August 1898.

S.S. Aberdeen

At Adelaide they ironically moved to the suburb York on the Port Road (near present-day suburb Beverley), having come from York in England. (The Port Road – now simply Port Road – was the major road between Port Adelaide and Adelaide city.) Just as he had done at Cherry Street, York, Arthur set up a bakery in front of the house on the corner of East Avenue.

Mary was to sadly die in 1901 of tuberculosis, less than three years after immigrating. She was buried at the nearby Cheltenham Cemetery. Arthur was devastated. He now faced with the prospect of bringing up five children alone. He was never to remarry.

Arthur with his five children

At the bakery on the Port Road it was reported that Arthur was fined for selling underweight bread. He was also fined for removing two swine from a quarantine district to the Adelaide Market. On the positive side it was reported that Arthur won prizes at the Hindmarsh Flower Show for roses and butter.

Arthur struggled with his business in difficult times and eventually went broke. He had to make a change, so moved with his son George to near Berri on the River Murray at the Riverland of South Australia. The River Murray is Australia's largest river. The constantly available water supply and sunny climate was a great boost for fruit growing on the banks of the river. Arthur built a solid brick house by the river near Berri. He mainly grew oranges and was said to have introduced the Valencia orange to the district.

Whenever Arthur visited his city-living children in Adelaide he would always bring a sugar bag full of oranges for the family. He made non-alcoholic wine for church communion and it was sold all over Australia. He also invented a mixture of dried fruits and coconut which he called "Little Normie." He had intended to go into partnership with Silas Martin, manager of The Ritz in Adelaide, to promote and sell the fruit candy. It did not eventuate.

At the Berri Royal Show Arthur won prizes for hens, eggs, vegetables, tomato sauce and best collection of citrus fruits. At the time he was the vice president of the Horticultural Agricultural Society and had become established in the Riverland district. He was an agent for Brock and Batchelor Ltd. (graders, packers and distributors).

In 1935 Arthur sailed travelling alone back to "the Mother Country" on the Otranto. It was his first return to England in nearly forty years. Strangely he visited his late wife's relatives rather than his own. (All of his siblings as well as his parents in England were by then dead. His only surviving sibling was his sister Sarah, who was in South Australia, having immigrated in 1915. Arthur being the youngest in the family was the only one apart from her still living. He could only have visited nieces and nephews accordingly in England, whom he mainly had only known as small children prior to him emigrating.)

Arthur in England with his wife's family

Arthur as guest of honour          Arthur at the cricket

He stayed with George Moore (his late wife's nephew) at Kippax (near Leeds), Yorkshire. His return saw him meet up with many of his late wife's relatives, culminating in a large family reunion with Arthur as the guest of honour. Although it was more than 35 years since Mary had died in Australia, perhaps it was the opportunity for her relatives to at last pass on their belated expressions of sympathy in person to Arthur regarding his loss. Being a keen cricket follower, his visit included a trip to the Headingly Cricket Ground in Leeds to see some cricket. (This was the ground where Sir Donald Bradman had set the world record for highest test match score a few years previously.) Arthur returned via Fremantle on the Otranto to Adelaide.

The Advertiser newspaper had a regular feature called "Out among the people." The reporter travelled the countryside interviewing local people. In 1939, he interviewed Arthur G. Jarvis, who was one of the pioneers of the Berri irrigation system. He was asked about the contrast of the present state of the River Murray with that of 1914, when rainfall in the catchment areas was even less than it had been the previous year of 1938. The following excerpt appeared in an edition of the newspaper in 1939, with Arthur's response:

I wonder if the fruit-growers along the river realize what a difference the locks have made. They have been assured of a complete water supply during the whole of the time when there has been little fresh water coming in. In 1914 we used a horse and dray across the river bed at Berri. Our house at Berri was built of bricks which we carried across in a sledge. We tried the dray, but it was too much for horse up the steep banks, so we used the sledge. My two boys used to ride a bicycle from Lyrup across the river to Berri. Then one day we thought that we might not have enough water to pump for household supplies, so we built a bank of sand bags across the river and it held up. It only lasted for a few days, for there was a storm up river and it came down with a good flow. Still I always remember how I once blocked the Murray and I wonder if any other individual has done that. With the reservoirs and locks we now have it will certainly never be done in the future.

Upon his return to Berri from overseas, Arthur realized he had enjoyed his break from working on the river so much that he started making plans for retirement. He tidied up his affairs in the Riverland and moved back to Adelaide, staying with his son William at Rosetta Street, West Croydon (not far from where he had had his baker shop on Port Road, York).

Arthur was to die at the age of 78 of carcinoma of the stomach and metastasis of the liver. He was buried at Cheltenham Cemetery on Port Road in a grave alongside his wife Mary. (The grave lease expired in 2000 and was then reused. The gravestone was photographed and then destroyed.) At the time of his death, he left five surviving children (one deceased), fourteen grandchildren and two great grandchildren. Strangely his death certificate stated he was the father of seven children. Who was the seventh? It remains a mystery.

As he had died in 1940, Arthur would not have had to cope with the tragic loss of his grandson killed two years later in the Second World War. The son of Arthur's second daughter Gertrude was Sergeant Pilot Mervyn J. H. Baillie.

After schooling at Woodville High School, Mervyn went to work at the State Savings Bank. Upon the outbreak of World War II, he left the bank branch at Port Lincoln and joined the Air Crew of the Royal Australian Air Force. He was trained as a pilot, became a sergeant and went to Egypt to join the Number Three Squadron, arriving in March 1941.

He flew many missions in North Africa, the Mediterranean and the Middle East and had flown many types of planes including the Tiger Moth, Wirraway, Magisters, Gauntlet, Kittyhawk, Mohawk, Harvard, Hurricane and Tomahawk. In Egypt he acted as an instructor for new pilots joining the Squadron, being the most experienced trainer at the field at El Ballah (only having been trained himself as a rookie pilot twelve months before).

On 13 April 1942, his parents (nearest next of kin) and also Miss J. C. Stephens of Croydon received the following telegraph:

> DEEPLY REGRET TO INFORM YOU THAT SERGEANT MERVYN J. H. BAILLIE IS REPORTED TO HAVE LOST HIS LIFE AS RESULT OF AIRCRAFT ACCIDENT IN THE MIDDLE EAST ON 11TH. APRIL 1942. THE AIR BOARD JOINS WITH THE AIR MINISTRY IN EXPRESSING PROFOUND SYMPATHY IN YOUR SAD BEREAVEMENT.

Sergeant Baillie had been making a solo non-operational test flight in a Tomahawk II with an Allison engine. A court of inquiry or investigation of flying accidents was undertaken to determine the cause of the crash. Obtained from the National Archives of Australia, the following edited and abridged excerpts of some witness statements are produced herein:

> 1st witness: "On the previous evening I did my daily inspection on this aircraft. It was serviceable and I signed the appropriate column in the form 770."

> 3rd witness: "I flew the aircraft on the previous day. It was normal in every way except the airspeed indicator appeared sluggish below 50 m.p.h. Just before the accident I saw the pilot do a slow roll at

approximately 5000 feet. Standard regulations say that no dog fighting or aerobatics will be done under 3000 feet. I can only suggest that he might have been doing slow flying to test the lower range of the air speed indicator."

5<sup>th</sup> witness: "I was in the watch office when the news of the crash came through, so I ordered out the fire engine and travelled with it to the scene of the accident. Owing to the soft sand it took fifteen minutes to reach the aircraft. The aircraft had gone straight in vertically and made a circular crater fifteen feet across and ten feet deep. The wreck was still burning, so fire crew attacked the flames with $CO_2$ gas and foam. There was no trace of the pilot or engine, just a pile of broken spars and metal rigging."

6<sup>th</sup> witness: "I saw the Tomahawk aircraft flying straight and level at 150 to 160 m.p.h. at 400 feet. Then I saw it drop its nose and its port wing and dive in a gradual turn to the left for about 100 feet. It then spun to the left, vertically. At about 50 feet the pilot apparently steadied the aircraft in the spin but it was still diving vertically. It dived into the ground and burst into flames."

9<sup>th</sup> witness: "I went to the scene of the crash in the ambulance and found the wreckage of the aircraft in a deep crater and still burning. Owing to the depth that the aircraft was buried it was impossible to recover the pilot's body. In my opinion there were no recoverable remains of the pilot. Death must have been instantaneous from multiple injuries."

The court found that:

> Sergeant Baillie was authorized to air test the aircraft.
>
> Excellent conditions, visibility 50 miles.
>
> Engine and airframe serviceable for the flight, fuel system cleaned.
>
> Pilot of average experience; 70 hours on operations, no previous accident.
>
> Aircraft too badly damaged to determine:
>
> (a) Structural failure.
>
> (b) Attempted parachute use.

In summary the court found that the error of judgement on part of the pilot followed by misuse of controls, which resulted in the aircraft spinning. The Commanding Officer and the Group Commander both concurred with the findings of the court.

The aircraft had been buried so deeply in the sand that Sergeant Baillie's body could not be recovered. The crash site was to be his grave at El Ballah. A funeral service was conducted at the crash site with many in attendance. The exact details regarding the circumstances of his burial (or non-burial), were never given to his family. They were only told the name of the burial location.

Sergeant Pilot Mervyn J. H. Baillie

## Conclusion:

## ARTHUR GISCARD JARVIS (1862 – 1940)

Just a name and a date? Research has shown that Arthur Giscard Jarvis was the youngest of a family of nine children born in Wisbech, Cambridgeshire in England. The family moved to York and following his father's death. Arthur married a servant girl Mary Moore and started a family. Having been taught the trade of being a baker/confectioner by his father, Arthur was quick to set up his own business. He had success with his bakery, showing sound business sense and a willingness to work hard. Subsequently, he was able to upgrade to a superior shop at Micklegate, a prime location.

Why did he come to Australia? Arthur's life was suddenly thrown into turmoil. One of his sons died and his wife was depressed and in poor health, unable to cope with the cold English weather. A major decision had to be made – quickly. Arthur committed to abandoning the successful bakery business and immigrated to Australia, in the hope that the better climate would be beneficial to Mary's failing health. This commitment was admirable as it showed his love and concern for Mary – which was much greater than for any of his business concerns.

All was in vain as Mary died a short time after arriving in South Australia. Arthur was devastated when she died. She had been the reason why the family had immigrated. He had to decide whether to return "home" to England or remain in Australia. He chose the latter, considering his children would have far more opportunities in Australia. He never remarried, but valiantly raised his five children by himself.

Arthur faced another challenge when he went bankrupt with the bakery business that he had established in South Australia. However, he had the determination and courage to start afresh growing oranges at Berri in the Riverland. With continual hard work ensuring success, he re-established himself and became an early pioneer in the district, a respected fruit grower and expert in irrigation in the Riverland. With his savings Arthur was able to make a trip to visit family in England. Upon return he was to retire to Adelaide and spent his final days living with his son, after having tidied up his affairs at Berri. Arthur died at the age of 78 years and was buried at the Cheltenham Cemetery alongside his beloved wife Mary.

In photographs, Arthur had the appearance of a dapper well-dressed Englishman, however he was one who could roll his sleeves up and get down to work when necessary. He had not saved his wife by coming to Australia, but he had been an excellent role model for his five children and established a positive future for them and their families.

He was my great grandfather.

Lomas Cottage at Rottnest Island

# 6

# JOHN BENEDICT LOMAS

## 1806 – 1888

# FAMILY TREE

Note: John Benedict Lomas was not a direct "blood" relative of mine, actually being a quite distant relative by marriage on my family tree.

However, he has been included in this book as he is a fine example of not just a "name and a date," but a person who has a story to tell.

The surname Lomas is a Spanish habitational name meaning "lived on a hill."

John Benedict Lomas was born in about 1806 in a farming community called Bishop Monkton, in North Yorkshire, England. He was christened on 29th October 1806 at St. Mary's Church at nearby Knaresborough. He was the first child and eldest son of Ralph Lomas and Elisabeth Horner. The family was Roman Catholic.

His father Ralph was a Second Lieutenant in the Royal Marines. He sent John for his schooling to the Ampleforth College in North Yorkshire, one of the foremost Catholic boarding schools in the country. It had opened in 1802 and was run by Benedictine Monks. His father had hoped that John may have become part of the religious order and join the monastery, however religion was not the thing for John. As a young man he was looking to lead a *much more* adventurous life.

Ampleforth College

At the age of sixteen John joined the English Army and was put in the Sixty Sixth (Berkshire) Regiment of Foot Division. He joined the Division at London, spent a short time at Edinburgh and then was transferred to Enniskillen in county Fermanagh in then Ireland (now Northern Ireland).

The Sixty Sixth (Berkshire) Regiment of Foot Division had previously been at St. Helena guarding the French military leader Napoleon Bonaparte who was imprisoned in exile after being defeated by the English at the Battle of Waterloo in 1815. When Napoleon died in 1821, six members of the Sixty Sixth Division carried him in his coffin to his tomb at St. Helena. (In 1840 his remains were relocated to France and were entombed in the Les Invalides at Paris.) Despite the dictator being thought of as a tyrant by most, the English Army recognized Napoleon as a great general and gave him a respectable funeral.

Sixty Sixth (Berkshire) Foot Division

John in later years was to claim that he was with the Sixty Sixth Regiment on St. Helena at that time. His claim was simply not true. He did not join the army until after that event. There would be a continuation of many claims and boasts which John made during his lifetime that were exaggerated, the truth stretched or more often completely false.

At Enniskillen in Ireland Private Lomas was soon to be in trouble. He deserted not once, but twice. (Desertion in the army had a penalty of death.) He was arrested and sent for court martial. It is not known whether, being of Roman Catholic faith, he was uncomfortable with the English army oppressing the Irish Roman Catholics, or (more likely) he was too young and not ready to handle the discipline of army life.

The court martial was held at Enniskillen in November 1823. At the age of seventeen, John Benedict Lomas was found guilty of twice deserting and was sentenced to seven years transportation to Australia. A description was given of the now army prisoner just before he set sail for Australia: age eighteen, height five foot six inches, complexion fair, hair brown, eyes hazel. Condition was listed as "well."

The military convict ship Ann and Amelia, under Captain Assough, transported John (and approximately 200 other convicts) from Cork to Sydney in a voyage of 116 days. They were guarded by the 40th (Foot) Regiment. They landed at Botany Bay in January 1825. The prisoners on board were treated harshly, and John at aged eighteen was mixing with many hardened criminals. He had to keep his wits about him and he learnt quickly. John had been corrupted by the criminals and had already formed a hatred for the authorities. It would stay with him for the remainder of his life.

The period of the 1820s and 1830s was a notorious time in the colony of New South Wales. Boatloads of convicted prisoners (both men and women) were being shipped from Britain to the other side of the world and being dumped on the shores. Many of those arriving had been transported for a minor indiscretion such as stealing a loaf of bread "because they were hungry," or stealing a silk handkerchief "because it was pretty." Others however were violent thugs, professional thieves, highwaymen or murderers, most of them being of extremely bad character. The prisons were crowded, the conditions were harsh and continual lawlessness and lack of control and discipline were evident. Prisoners would make escape attempts at any and every opportunity and John was no exception.

In the prison system, some convicts were sent to work in gangs building roads and bridges or were "signed on" to a local landowner. Being under less supervision, their opportunity for escape was increased and John made several escape attempts and committed various misdemeanours while on the run. When a convict did escape, to survive they often took to being a bushranger, not quite robbing the rich to feed the poor as Robin Hood did, but more to rob both the rich and the poor to feed themselves.

A convict ploughing team road gang

If escape attempts had been made and bushranger activities carried out, the authorities increased prison sentences and decreed sentences of hard labour to those recaptured (or on some occasions even sentences of death). There was strict discipline enforced for those who were sent back to prison and severe penalties if they did not comply with the rules. John was to experience all this.

Initially John was sent to Penrith, then sent to work on a road gang, which gave him an opportunity for his first of many escapes. When recaptured he was sentenced to three years further imprisonment and transferred to Port Macquarie on the Amity. He was to make several more escape attempts and in 1829 was listed as "a troublesome character," as while having absconded from the Hyde Park barracks in Sydney, he became drunk and insolent. He was charged with this in addition to his absconding charge, receiving a sentence of three months working on the road gang. Once on the road gang, a month later he again escaped!

To survive as an escapee, it was necessary for John to steal at any and every opportunity. He was arrested again for highway robbery and larceny of goods at Bathurst after an escape, accompanied by Jeremiah McCarthy. In court at Windsor, in early 1830 he and McCarthy were charged with highway robbery to a John Moore and a Henry Turner (separate incidents) at Bathurst. John Benedict Lomas was sentenced to death for highway robbery, McCarthy however was acquitted on that charge. On the larceny charges, stealing from William Lane and Jonathan Hassell, (separate incidents), both were found guilty and both Lomas and McCarthy were sentenced to an extra seven years prison.

John's sentence to death was commuted to the seven years jail to be served concurrently with the larceny charge. This sentence was in addition to John's other sentences still being served. In 1830 John was transferred to Moreton Bay Prison in Queensland on the Lucy Ann. Moreton Bay was considered a stricter prison with tighter security for convicts who had re-offended. John still managed to escape a further five times! (On one occasion, upon recapture, he was to receive 100 lashes as punishment.)

In 1837 John was returned to Sydney where he eventually was granted his pardon. (It had been fourteen years after his original seven years sentence in Ireland by the English Army to be transported to Australia.) Now he had his "certificate of freedom." Such an important document, yet he was to lose it!

Certificate of freedom

John with his newly attained freedom after fourteen years of incarceration, now had the opportunity to establish a new life for himself. He could marry, settle down, have a family. He was away from the hardened criminals he had mixed with for all his adult life up until then – but had he become one of them? The Colony offered many opportunities for him to start a new life if he wished.

Captain Charles Sturt

An announcement was made that the famous explorer Captain Charles Sturt was to lead a cattle drive overland from near Goulburn to Adelaide in the newly established colony of South Australia. (Captain Sturt eight years earlier in a whale boat had led an expedition down the Murray River to its mouth and then returned upstream, being the first to do so.) Sturt was no longer in the army having resigned. He had married and settled down in New South Wales at Belconnen (near present day Canberra) as a farmer. He had been almost ruined by a disastrous three years drought on his farm. His crops had failed and the cattle and sheep that he kept could not easily be driven to Sydney for sale at the markets due to the shortage of feed and water on the way. As well as this, the prices for livestock at the Sydney market were low. There was however an existing shortage of livestock at the markets in Adelaide. Almost in desperation, Captain Sturt embarked on an ambitious plan to drive his cattle overland to the new market. The feat had been accomplished recently a couple of times by others. They had their challenges yet managed to overcome them and reached their destination.

Giles Strangways                    Captain John Finnis

Captain Sturt formed a team "with the right stuff" for the anticipated challenging journey. They included a previous whaler Captain John Finnis (of the merchant service), Giles Strangways (whose brother was the acting temporary Colonial Secretary of Adelaide), Mr. Macleod (a friend from Norfolk Island), Mr. Fraser (a former soldier who accompanied Sturt on his Murray River expedition), Robert Flood (who later accompanied Sturt on his Central Australia expedition), a few stockmen and a former convict named Lomas.

How John Lomas had managed to be selected by Captain Sturt for the ambitious cattle drive is not known. John did possess the natural ability to "talk and persuade," a trait which many con men excelled in – or alternatively, Captain Sturt may have been unaware of the abysmal convict record of John Benedict Lomas, as he had not mentioned it in his job interview!

In 1838, Captain Sturt set off from Goulburn and followed the upper reaches of the Hume River in a westerly direction passing the Goulburn River junction. At Fowler's Station (near present day Albury) there was a general muster and from there he led the cattle drive comprising stock of three hundred cattle and thirty sheep. They continued on and when they reached Mount Hope, Captain Sturt was to lose his flock of thirty sheep when they were attacked and scattered by wild dogs. They then reached the junction of the Murrumbidgee River.

Up to then they had not had any major problems, (apart from losing the sheep), swimming the cattle across the river when required and using the dray as a punt. Captain Sturt was mapping the Hume River as he went, noting that in 250 miles there had been six tributaries running into the main river. Sturt was to come to the realization that the Hume River (named by Hamilton Hume in 1824) and the Murray River (named by himself in 1830) were in fact the same river.

There had been recent heavy rains in the catchment area and many logs were floating in the river. Dangerous snags were found below water level. Captain Sturt was to later make a report that he did not consider this section of the river to be suitable for the "medium of internal communication."

The cattle drive reached the junction of the River Darling. Here Finnis argued with Sturt that it was not necessary to completely dismantle the dray in order to cross the river. After some consideration, Sturt reluctantly acceded to Finnis and let him drive the fully loaded dray into the river crossing. It immediately became hopelessly bogged! Empty casks were used as buoyancy floats to eventually free the dray and it was pulled ashore using bullocks and ropes.

A copy of a sketch made by Sturt of the Murray/Darling rivers junction

While the cattle drive had been delayed and was in some disarray with the bogged dray, some aborigines entered the camp. There was an altercation and some blows were thrown and some blood spilt. (Lomas?). Captain Sturt intervened and they were then able to move on without further trouble.

Captain Sturt had noticed with concern that the aborigines that they had encountered on this trip were not quite the same as those he had come across on his River Murray expedition (to the mouth). They appeared to be not as friendly and were more cautious in their attitude. Later during the cattle drive a cow was speared and a drover's dog attacked. At one stage Captain Sturt found it necessary to make a temporary stockade with the dray to guard against a possible attack.

Captain Sturt also observed, much to his consternation, that the aborigines seemed to be less in number and appeared to have been significantly affected by disease, many having been permanently pitted by smallpox scars. (Captain Sturt was at the end of the trip to warn authorities in Adelaide that the aborigines were likely to cause problems and possibly become hostile in the near future – a prediction which came to fruition when many aborigines were slaughtered after killing some white people in the area.)

The party was running short of food supplies and Captain Sturt sent Strangways and Fraser ahead to bring back supplies to those herding the cattle. With Mt. Lofty in sight in the distance, their situation was becoming dire, however supplies were brought back to the main party. The cattle drive eventually reached Mount Barker in the Adelaide Hills, not far from

Adelaide. There was ample water and grassy grazing pastures there for the stock. The overland cattle drive had been accomplished in just over three months. (Captain Sturt had only mentioned Lomas once in his personal diary – when he sent him back to retrieve some missing cattle that had strayed away from the main herd.)

Following the completion of the cattle drive, John returned to Sydney. He had been shocked to find that his certificate of freedom went missing on his trip to South Australia while on the cattle drive. He needed his certificate as proof that he was no longer a convict and he had not escaped and was on the run. It was his gateway to freedom, to start out on a new life on the "straight and narrow."

John lodged the following paid advertisement in the Sydney Herald newspaper in November 1838:

NOTICE.

I HEREBY Caution all Constables and others not to molest me after this Notice, I having lost my Certificate of Freedom on my way to South Australia, in June last.

Description – Name, John Lomas; per ship Ann and Amelia; year of arrival, 1825; native place, Yorkshire; sentence, seven years; age, thirty-two; height, five feet seven and three-quarter inches; eyes, hazel; hair, brown; complexion, brown; sandy whiskers; general remarks, scar on the back of the right hand.

JOHN LOMAS.

John then returned to Adelaide and managed to get a job as a trooper in the South Australian Police Force. It was a time when conditions were difficult in the fledgling colony, being only about three years since it was established. How did an ex-convict and bushranger so readily gain a position as a policeman? Did Captain Sturt (who had sold his farm in New South Wales and was now living at Grange in Adelaide) put in a good word for him? Did John use his "gift of the gab" to gain the job? It is more likely that in those desperate times anyone, no matter what their background, would have been accepted for the position. South Australia, a free settlement, had already started to be overrun by bushrangers and escaped convicts from the colony of New South Wales to the east, as well as ship deserters. They were causing widespread havoc among the free settlers.

In 1840, Trooper Lomas was to receive some accolades for arresting a bushranger named Joseph Stagg (an escaped convict from Van Diemen's Land). In a mangrove swamp near the Para River, Stagg had murdered a fellow bushranger named John Gofton (who had previously escaped from captivity in Adelaide) by shooting him through the head. The two bushrangers had been pursued by the police for cattle stealing in the Black Forest area. The stolen cattle were being slaughtered, dressed and salted, with the intention to sell the beef illegally to sailing ships.

At the trial in Adelaide, Trooper Lomas gave evidence that he had arrested and helped convict the accused Stagg who was sentenced to death by hanging by a visibly upset Chief Justice Cooper. (The unpleasant judgement having to be made was his first sentence given for the death penalty.)

Stagg was duly hung at the new Adelaide Jail. (The first hanging carried out at the new jail.) He had continually maintained his innocence even when the noose was tightened and as the hanging was carried out. The story was to take an amazing turn about ten years later, causing an investigation and then the whole case to be reinvestigated in 1874. (See later.)

Jane Barnes met John Lomas in Adelaide. He was a smooth talker who said all the right things and promised her the world. He seemed to be a man of the world – who had experienced the world. He had a steady job as a police trooper. She was impressed, and he seemed to be a man she could settle down with. They married in 1840 at the Holy Trinity Church in North Terrace, Adelaide. John was 33 years of age and Jane was 16 years of age. (He was more than double her age.)

John and Jane were to have at least five children. A couple of children were given the Christian name of John's mother and a sister. Perhaps this was John's way of giving recognition to them, incorporating the names into his own children. John had left the family home at age sixteen to join the English Army. As he was transported to Australia direct from the Army, he would never have seen his younger siblings again and did not spend time growing up with them in their teenage years. Nor would he have seen his parents since joining the Army.

Jane (née Barnes) Lomas Day Kempster

After their marriage John resigned from the police force and began farming on land at Bexley near the Sturt River (near present day Marion). This period of married life with his family was probably the most stable part of John's lifetime – but it was not to last. In 1849, on North Terrace, Adelaide he was arrested for being drunk and disorderly. He denied being drunk but admitted to disorderly behaviour. He was fined five shillings by the court. Then the next month his daughter Margaret died at aged only 18 months of age. His life had started to unravel and spiral out of control as he displayed signs of mental deterioration.

A claim was made by John in the early 1850s that he received word of the ownership of the family farm in Yorkshire being disputed by his two younger brothers Thomas and Edward. It was common in those days for the family farm to be left by the father to the eldest son. (John was the eldest son.) John had left home however at the age of sixteen and had not returned to the family farm since. The younger two brothers worked and maintained the farm and, with John absent, took over the farm after their father's death in 1841. In John's mind he was entitled to the farm. He believed it was his inheritance, being the eldest son.

John left his wife (who was pregnant) and children, (saying he was going to Western Australia to find work). Instead of heading west, he sailed back to England to – in his mind – rightfully claim his inheritance. (His wife Jane was to later remarry in John's prolonged absence.)

Upon arrival in England John made his way to York where his widowed mother was living. (John made the claim that he walked from Newcastle-on-Tyne to York with the sustenance of only one pennyworth of bread.) While visiting his mother he was arrested when in the town for being drunk and disorderly and was fined five shillings. On this occasion he pleaded guilty to being disorderly and being drunk! His mother was not impressed and John was soon roaming the streets and country lanes by himself, finding accommodation wherever he could.

John sought out the perceived wrongs so that they could be righted, but in court it had been ruled that as the younger two brothers had made a full input to the upkeep of the farm, they were entitled to own it. Alone in England John was a shattered man. His mental health deteriorated further.

It was during this time that John was to make an extraordinary confession on the Wetherby to Collingham Road to a young police constable William

Eccles. John had surrendered himself to the policeman. He confessed that he had shot and killed a man eleven years ago when he was working as a police trooper in the colony of South Australia. In the voluntary statement (which he signed), he confessed that he had shot a prisoner, John Guyton, under his control for cattle stealing, knowing he was carrying a large quantity of gold sovereigns.

He himself had arrested Guyton's bushranger partner Joseph Stagg, who was charged with Guyton's murder, convicted and sentenced to hang. Stagg was subsequently executed, pleading his innocence till the end. The confession was made in such a precise and circumstantial manner that it was taken very seriously. (John Lomas was also to later make the same confession to George Hall, the governor at the Parkhurst Prison.)

A copy of the signed confession was sent by the Clerk to the Magistrate at Weatherby to the Governor of South Australia. The Governor ensured that in Adelaide the murder was re-investigated by the Trial Judge and the Police Commissioner. They visited the crime scene and re-interviewed witnesses who were still available to be interviewed. Damning evidence at the trial had been that only one set of footprints (apart from the victim's), had been found near the body by black trackers, indicating they were made by a splay-footed person who walked with his feet turned out, treading on one side of each foot. The footprints matched the boots which were found at Stagg's accommodation. Stagg had also been observed in the vicinity at the time carrying a gun. The conclusion that they came to was that the original court judgement against Stagg had been correct.

There were however some interesting sidelines about the case, apart from the usual run-of-the-mill rumours. The death penalty was controversial with some who were not in favour of capital punishment. It had also been the first execution carried out at the new Adelaide Jail. Some still considered the sentenced man may have been innocent – perhaps Guyton had taken his own life? A journalist had interviewed Stagg before he was executed and reported that he had admitted to many crimes (even some that had the death penalty), but steadfastly denied murdering his "mate." "I am quite content to die, but as an innocent man as to this crime. I have been a violent bad man, but I could not kill a friend."

The Police Inspector Alexander Tolmer (who was the boss of Lomas), said that Lomas continually kept yelling "Murder!" at night when asleep in his bed in the barracks. The constant cries interrupted the sleep of other troopers in the barracks. The Police Inspector also indicated that the manager of the South Australian Bank had confided to him that after the murder Lomas had deposited a considerable amount of gold into the bank, something that for a man on a basic policeman's meagre wage (five shillings per day) could not be explained. Lomas was also reported to have used abusive language to a superior officer. By mutual agreement between John and the Police Inspector, it was decided that it was in everyone's best interests that John resign from the Police Force.

Shortly after his confession, John was admitted to a lunatic asylum at Wakefield in England with a mental breakdown. After an examination he was classified as "insane, dangerous and suicidal." He had told them he was a soldier, even though he had been dismissed from the English Army nearly thirty years prior.

Eventually, John's condition improved and after a short-term trial release he was discharged permanently, being said to be "cured." To come to such a conclusion that he was sane and cured however was a huge misconception. Two months later he was sleeping in the open countryside near Whixley, Yorkshire. When he awoke from his sleep, for an unknown reason he set fire to a nearby barley stack and it burnt to the ground. He immediately gave himself up to the police.

The accused arsonist was taken to court at the Yorkshire Assizes in 1852. Lomas explained to the court that he set fire to the barley to rally his friends to arrange for his trip back to Australia. He was convicted and, for the second time in his life, was sentenced to transportation, this time for fifteen years. (It had been known on occasions for individuals to purposely commit a crime such as stealing a sheep to obtain a free passage to Australia. Whether John set fire to the barley as an attempt to get passage back to Australia is a possibility.)

Stirling Castle prison hulk at Portsmouth

John was continually transferred between various prisons and even spent time in the Stirling Castle, a prison hulk moored at the waterfront near Portsmouth. At the Stirling Castle it was reported that he was "of very irritable temper". He was also incarcerated at Wakefield, Millbank, and Dartmoor. He was regularly in and out of various mental institutions when his mental condition fluctuated. At one stage he was at the infamous Bethlem Royal Hospital (Bedlam Asylum) in London, which did however have a library, of which John took advantage. (Bethlem Hospital was the oldest psychiatric hospital in the world, being established in 1247.) He was transferred to a lunatic asylum in Salisbury, where he made an escape but was recaptured. Why was he in and out of institutions in different areas? This was a strange situation in an era when generally inmates were locked up, forgotten, and the key was thrown away. Perhaps his symptoms of illness were intermittent. Perhaps, as he was a smooth-talking con man, he was able to talk his way out. Perhaps it was an act and he wasn't ill at all!

Bethlem Royal Hospital

While in various prisons, John sent petitions to the Home Secretary asking to be pardoned and relocated to Australia, citing the situation that he had family there, as well as that he was of unsound mind when the arson was committed. (Once again it must be considered that his action in setting fire to the barley may have been a ruse to get transported back to his family in Australia.) His request wasn't granted.

John was sent again to Bethlem Hospital in London. (He was to be there on at least three occasions between 1854 and 1857.) There he was deemed by the Superintendent Dr. Charles Hood to be completely sane. His health and behaviour had markedly improved. The Superintendent had noted that previous displays of mental instability resulting in his transfer from jail to an asylum, often (coincidentally) ran in parallel with his sentences of having to do hard labour in prison.

As per his sentence to be transported for committing arson, in 1857, after five years from being sentenced, John was duly taken by the convict ship Clara I from London to Fremantle, Western Australia. He was accompanied by 261 other prisoners on a 106-day voyage. (The final convict ship to transport prisoners from England to Australia was in 1867.)

This time it was John as an older hardened criminal who was corrupting the younger convicts on board. Upon arrival he was kept in the Convict Establishment (which later in 1867 was renamed the Fremantle Prison). At one stage he refused to eat for eleven days, eventually having to be force-fed. His stay at the jail was regularly interrupted by visits to the Fremantle Lunatic Asylum. John's mental health ebbed and flowed like the tide at the Fremantle Port.

A "ticket of leave" was received by John, meaning he could find paid work away from the prison but was not allowed to go from his allocated district. He was soon arrested near Albany on his way to Adelaide to meet up with his family, being out of his allocated district. In 1860, John received a conditional pardon (this time not misplacing it). He went to the Benedictine Monastery at New Norcia but was unable to procure regular work. His freedom was short lived however, as in 1861 he was arrested in Albany and convicted for stealing a horse, once again attempting to return to his family in Adelaide. A ten-year sentence given at the Albany court was the result.

John escaped jail in 1864 and headed north. Somehow obtaining a gun, he began robbing shepherds and farmers. He was recaptured near the New Norcia monastery, and it was suggested that he would be more suited to a lunatic asylum than a prison. His mental state had again deteriorated. He was given a new ticket of leave, but once again was arrested having absconded outside of his allocated territory and was returned to jail, being sentenced to six months of hard labour. His ticket of leave was cancelled due to his mental condition and he was transferred to the lunatic asylum at Fremantle.

A description of John was recorded by the Fremantle Prison. As compared to the description of him as a young man, he was still the same height, same hazel eyes, but now with greying hair and was "middling stout," obviously due to his increase in age since the original description of him after his court martial when he was in the English Army.

In 1869, a new governor was appointed in Western Australia, being Sir Frederick Weld. He was a Roman Catholic and became acquainted with John at a church service. Being the smooth-talking con man that he was, John befriended the approachable Governor. In 1870 Governor Weld granted his fellow Roman Catholic a free pardon.

Through the insistence of Governor Weld, the authorities were asked to find suitable employment for John and for him to be taken care of. Many attempts were made to find permanent employment for him – but they were not successful.

The authorities through the Colonial Secretary then made a somewhat amazing decision. They decided to build, (constructed by prison labourers), a single room limestone cottage with shingle roof and a fireplace on Rottnest Island for John to live. (A request had been made by John to Governor Weld that he wished to spend his final days on Rottnest Island.) He was to have free privileges, free supplies, and could grow his own vegetables in a garden at the cottage. (Most other occupants of Rottnest Island – mainly aboriginal prisoners – were treated badly and fed bread and water.)

John was supplied food and clothing and was also given a daily ration of two ounces of rum as a stimulant. He was permitted to go to the mainland on occasions, attending church services, keeping doctor's appointments and, whenever it was possible, visiting his friend and protector Governor Weld. (Governor Weld kindly supplied John with snuff on each visit.) John was referred to as the "Imperial Pauper" at Rottnest Island. The newspapers generally referred to him as "Captain Lomas" from his bushranger days. He continued to struggle with his mental condition.

Sir Frederick Weld

In 1874 John left Rottnest Island, having convinced the authorities to allow him to return to Adelaide to "clear his name." He also wanted to see his family, having in 1872 put a "missing friends" advertisement (which was unanswered) in the Adelaide Police Gazette. He travelled by steamer ship the Georgette from Fremantle to Adelaide, a determined perceived victim on a mission.

It was reported in the South Australian Register under the heading "Strange Story." Here are some edited extracts:

> That Adelaide had been visited by a man known in the Colony as a notorious convict, of eccentric habits, who seems to have very successfully imposed on our contemporary with his plausible yarn.

> The fellow introduced himself into Adelaide's society as a man of property, and had created for himself a new office under our local Government as Minister of Mines. His ostensible reason for coming here he alleges to that he may clear himself of imputation which has been allowed to go uncontradicted for over a quarter of a century, namely, that he murdered a man for whose death another person in 1840 suffered the extreme penalty of the law.

In John's claim to the newspaper, he was adamant that he had not killed the bushranger, as he had no motive and money was found to still be on the bushranger's dead body (thirteen pounds worth of gold). Upon the claimed confession attributed to him in England, John denied making any confession and claimed to only have read about it in an English newspaper which reported that he had confessed and died as a lunatic.

An enquiry was ordered by the Governor to be conducted by Judge Crawford. Evidence was taken from those who were still able to attend (being almost 35 years after the event). The court then moved to the actual murder scene and the murder was re-enacted. Although the senior sergeant at the time did acknowledge that Trooper Lomas had been ordered to go for rations on that particular evening, it was found that the spot where Lomas had indicated where he had shot the bushranger was in fact three quarter of a mile and several small salt-water creek crossings from where the body was found. It would have been impossible for Lomas to drag the dead body that distance. It was also considered that one of the other policemen would have heard the sound of the shot if it had been fired from where Lomas had indicated that the shooting took place.

Judge Crawford, after examining the evidence, concluded, "The confession by Lomas was a gross fabrication. A most inexplicable circumstance by Lomas in returning to South Australia after charging himself with the crime."

After the court case, John Lomas indicated that he would return to Western Australia. He claimed that he had secured an island where he hoped to live and die like a "Robinson Crusoe."

While he was in Adelaide, John called to visit his wife Jane and his children, having abandoned them over twenty years prior. His offer to return and protect his wife and family was firmly rejected. His wife Jane had remarried again (her third husband) and had completely washed her hands of John, even though he was the actual father of her children. Her third husband George Kempster (an ex-policeman) was not welcoming to the interloper.

This rejection was not taken well by John. In the following year he was arrested and put in the dock for sending a threatening letter to George Kempster, mattress maker of King William Street, Adelaide. It read:

> Sir – You by your conduct towards me have made me your eternal enemy. I have received information that you have instigated my wife, to whom you are married, to disown me, and by that means my children will not own me. I am determined to have redress. I hereby give you notice that I will shoot you, so be prepared for the event. I am at the present moment almost deranged. I am at present distracted, and I assure you that your life or mine must fall a victim. I am confident that you are a villain, so expect your doom.
> I remain Sir, your enemy,
> John B. Lomas.

Lomas admitted to the court that he had written the letter under "circumstances of excitement." He stated that he had returned to the Colony of South Australia after 24 years. He had written the letter upon the misguided impression that he would receive justice in court. The judge Justice Waring reminded him that his action could bring punishment of life imprisonment. Lomas withdrew his plea of not guilty. He said that he wouldn't live long, and it didn't matter what would become of him. The judge asked whether he would annoy the prosecutor anymore. Lomas steadfastly answered "Never." Considering the circumstance, the judge ordered seven days imprisonment with hard labour.

Once again John was to return to Western Australia, not to his "Robinson Crusoe" island, but to Rottnest Island. His reputation as the notorious "Captain Lomas" occasionally got him into the newspapers. In 1874, he was erroneously named in one newspaper (the Perth Gazette) as the person who in 1855 shot and killed Constable Knibbs, a policeman guard of the Albany mail on the road to Albany. The actual killer was Obadiah Stevens, a prisoner from the Albany Jail who was being transported to the Perth Hospital for medical treatment – not John Benedict Lomas, but another "lunatic prisoner." John was in this case a victim of mistaken identity and his own notoriety.

At Rottnest Island John was unsettled and not well behaved. There were instances of some of the male prisoners being swindled, and foul language being used at women. On one occasion he argued with the chief pilot of the island and threatened to cut his head open with a spade. The order was made that John was to leave Rottnest Island. His protector Governor Weld was no longer in Western Australia, as in 1874 he was transferred to Tasmania to become governor of that Colony. A distraught John was forcibly taken from his cottage kicking and screaming to the mainland.

John, the "wandering lunatic," again went out into the bush where he continued his usual activities. He robbed from many shepherds' huts and farmers' properties. Apart from the usual foodstuffs, guns, ammunition, tobacco and clothing, he stole books such as novels by Sir Walter Scott and various seafaring yarns. Apparently, when he was alone enjoying some solitude, being well educated, he liked to read. After this crime spree, John was arrested. Due to lack of evidence, he was acquitted, (not having any stolen goods in his possession. He had dumped the Sir Walter Scott and seafaring yarns books once he had read them.) He was, however, sentenced to a month of hard labour at Perth Jail for vagrancy.

Upon release John had nowhere to go. He was definitely not welcome at Rottnest Island. The Benedictine Monastery Community at New Norcia (where he had previously tried to find work) did not want him in any of their cottages, even after the Government had offered to reimburse them by one shilling per day. (The Benedictine Bishop later commented that even if the Government reimbursed them to take Lomas at *one pound per hour,* he would not take him in! He described him as a "first-class vagabond" and said he was "one quarter crazy and three quarters rogue.")

A short time was spent in the Mount Eliza Poorhouse, but John was soon back in the invalid depot at Fremantle. In 1885, he was arrested for stealing from a hut (at aged 79 years) and jailed for twelve months in Perth Jail, where he gave his occupation as "labourer, formerly a soldier." Upon release, he wrote a letter requesting a return to Rottnest Island. The Superintendent at Rottnest Island replied that the cottage was occupied by someone else, but even if it wasn't, Lomas was the last person he wanted to see on the island.

John's final years followed a familiar, depressing pattern: picked up for vagrancy, appearing in court, sent to jail, transferred to his "home away from home," the mental asylum. An old and defeated man, John continued aimlessly to roam the streets, alone and shuffling along in his tattered clothes, a forlorn figure in anonymity. He was continually jailed for vagrancy. The glory days of being in the English Army, supposedly guarding Napoleon, Captain Lomas the bushranger, overlander with Captain Sturt, Police Trooper Lomas and his friendship with Governor Sir Frederick Weld, were all a distant memory.

In 1888, John was again arrested for vagrancy, having absconded from York Hospital and being found rain-soaked in the open suffering from exposure. He appeared in the court in a distressed state and requested that the magistrate sentence him to prison and send him to his cottage on Rottnest Island, as he would be better there than anywhere else. This request was refused as the Magistrate said the cottage was being used for other purposes. (The cottage had been occupied by a warder on Rottnest Island named Buckingham. It was then referred to as "Buckingham Palace," however nowadays is known as "Lomas Cottage".) A dejected Lomas seemed very disappointed at this request being denied.

The magistrate sentenced Lomas to three months imprisonment. To this Lomas replied, "Thank you, Sir. I don't think I will ever trouble you again. My days are fast drawing to a close." These words were to be prophetic as a couple of months later John Benedict Lomas died in the Fremantle Prison Hospital. He was still serving his three months term for his final vagrancy charge.

An inquest was held on the following day concerning his death, before Mr. B. Fairbairn and a three-man jury. It was stated that Lomas had come to the colony of Western Australia in 1857. (There was no mention of his previous transportation to New South Wales.) It was said he had been a bushranger in Tasmania. He had given prison officials much trouble by his attempts to seize every opportunity to escape. Notwithstanding attempts by several philanthropists to persuade him to lead a respectable life, he preferred roaming about the bush pilfering and thieving whatever he could. He was said to be a very intelligent man, having evidently been well brought up and apparently educated. He had travelled all over the colonies of Australia and must have possessed a wonderful constitution to withstand the various hardships he experienced and to have lived to such an age.

The gatehouse old Fremantle Prison

The medical certificate showed that he suffered from indigestion and he died from old age and faulty digestion. The jury returned a verdict of death by natural causes. He was 82 years of age. He was buried in a pauper's grave at Fremantle.

Conclusion:

## JOHN BENEDICT LOMAS (1806 – 1888)

Just a name and a date? Research has shown that John Benedict Lomas was born in Yorkshire, England as the eldest of five children. Being a Roman Catholic, his father sent him to a boarding school run by the Benedictine Monks. Not interested in the Church, John was looking for adventure.

Why did he come to Australia? He had no choice. At sixteen he joined the English Army, was sent to Ireland and was court martialled for twice deserting. Found guilty, punishment was transportation to Australia for seven years.

So began the remarkable (and perhaps flawed) life of John Benedict Lomas in Australia.

What a conundrum!

What an enigma!

Was Lomas a complete villain? "Captain Lomas" had a record of army desertion, escaping prison, committing bushranger acts (including armed robbery), wife desertion, arson, threatening life, drunkenness, vagrancy and – if his confession is to be believed – murder.

Was he a very clever con man? He certainly had the "gift of the gab," was intelligent, well educated, not lacking in confidence and was able to persuade authorities as high as the Colonial Secretary and Governor of the Colony to agree to his whims.

Was he mentally unstable and delusional? He was continually admitted to mental asylums showing signs of instability and insanity. Remarkably he was then released, at a time when most mental patients were locked away in cells forever and the key thrown away. (The Superintendent at Bethlem Hospital in London, however, shrewdly observed that his admission to mental institutions, showing signs of insanity, generally coincided with his doing hard labour in prison. He declared him sane.)

The surprising decision to build "Lomas Cottage" on Rottnest Island must be considered. Many convicts had been executed for lesser crimes than the many that Lomas committed. Yet the cottage was built for him and he was given special privileges, while convicts on the island were in chains and fed bread and water.

Lomas had sentences reduced, a death sentence overturned and received free pardons. Why? It has been sensationally suggested that John Lomas may have been the illegitimate son of a very important person in England – dare we say, even *Royalty*! (He was referred to as the "Imperial Pauper" at Rottnest Island.) Perhaps this contributed to his continual receiving of privileges and concessions from the higher authorities.

My conclusion is that the eccentric John Lomas was an intelligent and educated man who when young made some poor decisions which led him to mix with hardened criminals until he became one of them. Crime became a way of life. He did have the ability to con and persuade, to gain privileges which the average (uneducated) convict could not attain. For a while (to his credit), he did attempt to go on the "straight and narrow," going on a cattle-drive with Captain Sturt, being a Police Trooper and marrying, raising a family and working on a farm.

This did not last as he suffered from periodic mental setbacks. He was at times delusional, as indicated by his claim to have guarded Napoleon, his perceived family inheritance, his confession to murder and his claim to own a "Robinson Crusoe" island. I do not consider that he was an illegitimate child of Royalty, but his ability to maintain relationships with authorities, particularly his friendship with his fellow Roman Catholic, the Governor of Western Australia, paved the way for reduced sentences, pardons and the building of his accommodation cottage at Rottnest Island.

Lomas lived out his life with prison sentences, escapes, mental asylum visits and as a vagrant on the streets. He finished up as a pauper, a lonely, frail old man charged one last time as a vagrant, then dying in the Fremantle Prison Hospital while serving his final sentence. He was 82 years of age.

He was the first husband of the wife of my fourth great uncle.

*A life that is not documented is a life that within a generation or two will largely be lost to memory. What a tragedy this can be in the history of a family. Knowledge of our ancestors shapes us and instils within us values that give direction and meaning to our lives.*

*- Dennis B. Neuenschwander*

Ron Dearing in his younger days

# AUTHOR'S NOTE

This book has been written to the best of my ability to give information which I believe to be correct, based on nearly two decades of research into my family tree. However, such things as personal letters, for example, are written by others expressing their own opinions (which is what they believe, but may not be necessarily be a correct belief). I have also included information from various newspapers, which can at times be reported without fully accurate details. My conclusions are those I have come to, my personal opinion expressed as I see it. I am grateful for the many people and organizations that have assisted me in various ways (see Acknowledgements). If I have misinterpreted any information that I have received or accessed, or have not given appropriate acknowledgement, I hereby apologize.

Ron Dearing

# ACKNOWLEDGEMENTS

I wish to acknowledge and express my deep appreciation and thanks to the so many wonderful people who have helped me in so many ways in writing this book, both recently and also with research in previous years.

Dr. Robert Ali, Adelaide, South Australia

Ian Bartlett, Adelaide, South Australia

Kathleen Bartlett*, Adelaide, South Australia

Pauline Bartlett*, Adelaide, South Australia

Brian Collard, West Yorkshire, England

Robyn Dearing, Adelaide, South Australia

Dr. Todd Dearing, Adelaide, South Australia

Roger Grigg, Adelaide, South Australia

Malcolm Healey, Adelaide, South Australia

Paul Jennings*, Cornwall, England

Ron Langhans, Sydney, New South Wales

Judith Lydeamore, Adelaide, South Australia

Leon Noble, Adelaide, South Australia

Mervyn Robinson, Adelaide, South Australia

Trevor Sherman, Northamptonshire, England

* deceased

I also wish to acknowledge the assistance of staff at the Mitcham Local History Service, the State Library of South Australia, and also Trove at the National Library of Australia.

# LIST OF PHOTOS

Photos included in this book have been supplied by myself, except those listed below, which I have been able to identify and hereby acknowledge.

Page 11     General Register Office England and Wales / Crown copyright MXA 453647

Page 12     Malcolm Healey

Page 17     The Illustrated London News / January 1849

Page 24     State Library SA PRG280/1/38/110

Page 25     C. A. Petts / Mitcham Local History Service

Page 26     C. A. Petts / Mitcham Local History Service

Page 27     Malcolm Healey

Page 40     Tower Hamlets Local History / ref. no P12563 class no. 331.1 / 040 / Cassell & Co.

Page 46     Ancestryimages.com

Page 48     Peter Higginbotham / The Workhouse

Page 55     Church Bells' Album of notable churches of the city of London 1891 by anonymous. Isham Books 2013

Page 74     Creative Commons / Gorredijk brug 04 / by TUFOWSKTM / licence CC BY 3.0

Page 108    (top left) Paul Jennings

Page 138    The Chronicle / Adelaide newspaper September 1911

Page 150    Brian Collard

Page 153    Historia y Arqueologia Maritima, University of Cadiz

Page 156    Brian Collard

Page 157    (left) Brian Collard

# BIBLIOGRAPHY

*Ancestry.com.au*. Ancestry Ireland Unlimited Company, 2021, www.ancestry.com.au.

Bull, John Wrathall. *Early Experiences of Colonial Life in South Australia*. Adelaide: Printed at the Advertiser, Chronicle, and Express Offices, 1878.

Capper, John. *The Emigrant's Guide to Australia*. London: George Philip & Son, 1853.

Cummings, Diane. 'Bound for South Australia: Passenger Lists 1836-1851.' State Library of South Australia, 2010-2017, bound-for-south-australia.collections.slsa.sa.gov.au.

Errington, Steve. 'The Life and Crimes of John Benedict Lomas.' *Early Days: Journal of the Royal Western Australian Historical Society*, vol. 14, no. 3, 2014, pp. 309-327.

*Family Search*. The Church of the Latter-Day Saints, 2021, www.familysearch.org.

*Genealogy SA*. Society Library and Research Centre, Genealogy SA, 2021, www.genealogysa.org.au.

Greville, Charles. *The Diaries of Charles Greville*. Random House, 2006.

Hallack, E. H. *Toilers of the hills, Part 2, South of Mount Lofty*. Curated by Judith Lydeamore. Upper Sturt, South Australia: Judith Lydeamore, 2019.

*Het Scheepvaartmuseum*. The National Maritime Museum, Amsterdam, Netherlands, 2017, www.hetscheepvaartmuseum.com/.

Hollingshead, John. 'Ragged London in 1861.' *Morning Post*, January 1861. London: Smith, Elder and co.

Jennings, Paul. Letter, February 2006.

*National Archives of Australia.* Australian Government, 2021, www.naa.gov.au/.

Num, Cora. *Convict Records in Australia.* Cora Num, 2007.

*Police Gazettes* (SA, Vic, NSW, WA), State Library of South Australia, 1862-, 1853-, 1854-, 1876-, Electronic Resource.

Purkis, Lottie (née Foster). Letter, 1990s.

Slater, Harold. Letter, 'Family Snippets – Those Remembered by Harold Slater.'

'Sturt's Forgotten Journeys of 1838.' The Charles Sturt Museum, www.charlessturtmuseum.com.au/resources/booklets/sturt%27s%20forgotten%20journeys%20of%201838.pdf.

Swiggum, S. and M. Kohli. *The Ships List: Passengers, Ships, Shipwrecks*, 2019, www.theshipslist.com.

*The Lancet*, www.thelancet.com/.

*The National Archives.* Government of the United Kingdom, 2021, www.nationalarchives.gov.uk/.

'Who Do You Think You Are.' Narrated by Richard Mellick. SBS, 2008-2021, www.sbs.com.au/ondemand/program/who-do-you-think-you-are.

*Wikipedia.* Wikimedia Foundation, 2021, www.wikipedia.org.

*Wikitree: Where Genealogists Collaborate.* Interesting.com, 2021, www.wikitree.com.

www.ingramcontent.com/pod-product-compliance
Lightning Source LLC
Chambersburg PA
CBHW060459290526
45791CB00001B/180